RIGHTSIDE-UP

LIVING IN AN

UPSIDE-DOWN

WORLD

— DAVID GIBSON

21st CENTURY CHRISTIAN

ISBN: 978-0-89098-913-5

©2016 by 21st Century Christian

2809 12th Ave S, Nashville, TN 37204

All rights reserved.

Cover design by Jonathan Edelhuber

Dedications

Dedicated to the memory of my parents,
John Paul and Esther Gibson,
who taught me and showed me the Way.

Acknowledgments

I wish to express my sincere appreciation to Frazier Conley for his valuable input in reviewing the manuscript of this book. The final product reflects many of his suggestions. Thanks to Hilary Ray for her computer skills in developing the graphics illustrating Luke 15:11-32 and Philippians 2:5-11. Thanks to Charles Brookshire and Mark McCallon, university research librarians, for their assistance in locating original sources for several quotations. I am also indebted to the authors and publishers who graciously granted permission to use their material, which has greatly enhanced this book.

Preface

When my 2½-year-old granddaughter wants me to read to her, I sometimes begin by turning the book upside-down, just to see her reaction. Always, she turns it right-side-up. She knows the difference.

When I was small, I recall lying on the couch with my head hanging chin-up over the side so I could view the living room from that strange angle. It was fascinating for a while, but soon I brought my head upright. Upside-down was not my preferred perspective.

Tragically, so much in our world today is upside-down: unworthy conceptions of God and of Jesus, unbiblical theories about the origin of the world and of human life, faulty ideas about truth and of Scripture, skewed views on what is considered moral behavior, misplaced priorities, false worship—and the list goes on.

Because upside-down is all that many people have ever known, a topsy-turvy world seems quite normal and natural. Anyone who dares to say otherwise is often met with considerable resistance from those who don't want their personal world turned over. They are comfortable as they are and wish only to be left alone. Peter addresses former pagans who have become disciples of Jesus Christ:

> As obedient children, do not be conformed to the former lusts which were yours in your ignorance, but like the Holy One who called you, be holy yourselves also in all your behavior; because it is written, "You shall be holy, for I am holy" (1 Peter 1:14-16).

Therefore, since Christ has suffered in the flesh, arm yourselves also with the same purpose, because he who has suffered in the flesh has ceased from sin, so as to live the rest of the time in the flesh no longer for the lusts of men, but for the will of God. For the time already past is sufficient for you to have carried out the desire of the Gentiles, having pursued a course of sensuality, lusts drunkenness, carousing, drinking parties and abominable idolatries. In all this, they are surprised that you do not run with them into the same excesses of dissipation, and they malign you; but they will give account to Him who is ready to judge the living and the dead (1 Peter 4:1-5).

Beloved, I urge you as aliens and strangers to abstain from fleshly lusts which wage war against the soul. Keep your behavior excellent among the Gentiles, so that in the thing in which they slander you as evildoers, they may because of your good deeds, as they observe them, glorify God in the day of visitation (1 Peter 2:11-12).

Now that these disciples are learning how to live right-side up, Peter urges them not to revert to their old upside-down ways by indulging the flesh as they once did. Their former comrades-in-sin cannot comprehend what in the world has come over these people. And what they cannot understand, they badmouth. Satan can use both the magnetic pull of old habits and the naysaying of former peers to pull the newly converted back down to where they once were. But a healthy appreciation for the benefits of right-side-up living helps keep one's head heaven-oriented and one's feet firmly planted on the foundation of Christ. Living upside down is no longer an option.

Right-side-up living has another advantage. Unbelievers who slander what they cannot comprehend cannot help but notice, and even admire, the good deeds they observe in believers. Their initial opposition may in some cases be replaced with openness to truth. A life turned right-side-up gets attention because it stands out in the crowd. Such a life can potentially change minds and open hearts previously closed to the truth.

The book you are about to read is designed to show the stark contrast between these opposite lifestyles—and why right-side up has all the advantages that upside down never had.

Table of Contents

Introduction

Fired for wasting supplies and facing an uncertain future, the manager ran through his options. Manual labor? Too hard. Begging? Too humiliating. But then the solution occurred to him: "I know what I shall do, so that when I am removed from the management people will welcome me into their homes."

By devising a clever plan of settling accounts by granting huge discounts to those who owed his boss, he created for himself a support group after he was out of a job. Those to whom he had given a break would "owe him one."

Jesus believed we can learn something from this resourceful fellow's networking:

> . . . the sons of this age are more shrewd in relation to their own kind than the sons of light. And I say to you, make friends for yourselves by means of the wealth of unrighteousness, so that when it fails, they will receive you into the eternal dwellings (Luke 16:8-9).

This savvy manager understood human nature and how to work the system, and so by helping others he helped himself. Likewise, Jesus says, when we give to others in this life, we insure for ourselves a warm welcome on the other side. In other words, working the system God's way pays big dividends in the long run. But is thinking about our reward unworthy of Christians?

Why We Do What We Do

Certainly, love of God should be our primary motive (1 John 5:3). Fear of hell is another incentive (Matthew 10:28). But should hope of reward play any part at all in our response to God's grace? Let's consider the evidence:

> But when you give to the poor, do not let your left hand know what your right hand is doing, so that your giving will be in secret; and your Father who sees what is done in secret **will reward you** (Matthew 6:3-4, emphasis added).

> But love your enemies, and do good, and lend, expecting nothing in return; and **your reward will be great** . . . (Luke 6:35).

> But when you give a reception, invite the poor, the crippled, the lame, the blind, and **you will be blessed**, since they do not have the means to repay you; for **you will be repaid** at the resurrection of the righteous (Luke 14:13-14).

> For I am already being poured out as a drink offering, and the time of my departure has come. I have fought the good fight, I have finished the course, I have kept the faith; in the future there is laid up for me **the crown of righteousness**, which the Lord, the righteous Judge, will award to me on that day; and not only to me, but also to all who have loved His appearing (2 Timothy 4:6-8).

> By faith Moses, when he had grown up, refused to be called the son of Pharaoh's daughter, choosing rather to endure ill-treatment with the people of God than to enjoy the passing pleasures of sin, **considering the reproach of Christ greater riches than the treasures of Egypt; for he was looking to the reward** (Hebrews 11:24-26, emphasis added).

For All the Right Reasons

Why was Moses willing to endure the heartaches of shepherding Israel who often resisted his leadership? Because he was totally convinced it was worth it. The last passage above says he did this "by faith." He truly trusted God to reward him.

The person who is highly motivated by God's rewards actually demonstrates great faith in God's power and promises. We honor God when we trust Him that much. We trust Him to do exactly what He said He would do. It's not that we deserve our reward or could ever earn it—it's all by His grace—yet we must fulfill our end of the bargain if we want God's greatest blessings.

Leon Morris provides a helpful corrective to a common misconception:

> The modern distaste for mentioning rewards and punishments is not shared by the NT writers. It is very true that it is never suggested that we serve simply to be rewarded. This is not a Christian attitude. The service we render God is that which springs naturally from the gratitude of redeemed hearts. But God will reward those who serve Him faithfully, and no NT writer appears to think this a thought for which he should apologize.[1]

Here Morris strikes a happy medium between two extremes: 1) doing what we do with only the reward in view and 2) thinking that reward should play no part in our motivation.

Cooperating with Nature

How has God designed things so that we can work in harmony with His arrangements and receive our reward? In the physical realm we study what we call the laws of nature so that we can use to our advantage such principles as gravity, osmosis, oxidation, photosynthesis, centrifugal force, inertia, aerodynamics, magnetism, electricity, etc. The fixed laws of our universe provide predictable structure and order to our lives. We don't wake up each morning to a bewildering new array of natural laws. Up has always been up; down is still down. Heat expands, cold contracts, just as always. Water continues to seek its own level; it evaporates, condenses, hardens into ice, and turns to steam, just as God designed it to do in the beginning.

Henry Eli Speck Sr. writes:

> The order which so definitely runs through the entire universe is maintained through the operation of law. If this were not true, we would have a chance universe. Because the sun rose yesterday would be no reason to expect it to do so today. The sun might come up in the west instead of the east, and it might

set a few moments after it arose. One might be lighter than air at one time and many times more dense at another. Man as a rational being must be able, however, to depend upon nature for continuity. The principle of continuity is an expression of our trust in nature that she will keep her promises.[2]

No doubt, Speck would have agreed, it is not nature as such that we should trust for keeping promises, but the *God* of nature. As M. H. Cressey observes:

"Natural laws" are descriptions of that universe in which God is ever at work. It is only by an unwarranted philosophical twist that they are construed as the self-sustaining working of a closed system or the rigid decrees of a God who set the universe to work like some piece of machinery.[3]

Rather, God continues to keep the promise He made to Noah after the Flood:

> While the earth remains,
> Seedtime and harvest,
> And cold and heat,
> And summer and winter,
> And day and night
> Shall not cease (Genesis 8:22).

Summer and winter and springtime and harvest,
Sun, moon and stars in their courses above
Join with all nature in manifold witness
To Thy great faithfulness, mercy and love.[4]

We serve a God of order. He designed the universe in such a way that astronomers can predict with precision the timing and viewing location of the next solar eclipse. The ebb and flow of the tides, the phases of the moon, the migratory pattern of Monarch butterflies, the hibernating habits of forest creatures, the delicate symmetry of the snowflake, the marvels of the genetic code, the spawning of the salmon—all these are the handiwork of the God who keeps it all in motion, just as He designed it.

In view of how God continues to govern His universe in a consistent, orderly way (Jeremiah 33:20-21, 25-26), does it seem reasonable that He would operate the spiritual realm haphazardly? It is reassuring to know that His principles for our spiritual good are just as definite, predictable, and knowable as any law of His physical creation. And they work just as well today as they did in Bible times. Human nature hasn't changed, God has not changed, and God's plan for us imperfect humans still works!

Cooperating With God

What is God's *modus operandi*—that is, by what method does He operate in our world? Exactly how does God work in our lives? How can we live in a way that harmonizes with His will? And how can we avoid the pitfalls that hinder our relationship with Him?

This study features thirteen spiritual principles by which God relates to us—and by which we can cooperate with Him. As Howard and William Hendricks define it, "A principle is a succinct statement of a universal truth."[5] Stephen R. Covey explains how it works:

> Principles are deep, fundamental truths, classic truths, generic common denominators. They are tightly interwoven threads running with exactness, consistency, beauty, and strength through the fabric of life.
>
> Even in the midst of people or circumstances that seem to ignore the principles, we can be secure in the knowledge that principles are bigger than people or circumstances, and that thousands of years of history have seen them triumph, time and time again. Even more important, we can be secure in the knowledge that we can validate them in our own lives, by our own experience.[6]

These principles have built-in rewards for those who live in harmony with them, and built-in penalties for those who ignore them, as Speck says:

> It is impossible to live as a physical being in the natural world

in violation of or in disregard to the physical laws without suffering the consequences. The same is true of life in the spiritual realm . . . . The laws are just as dependable, as reliable, as absolute in one realm as in the other.[7]

Wouldn't it be to our advantage to be as familiar with these principles as we are with the law of gravity? If God expects us to learn how to use natural laws to our advantage, wouldn't He want us to do the same with His spiritual laws? Joe Barnett writes:

God didn't put laws into the Bible so he could catch us when we break them, but because they reflect the way life works.

For example, God instructed children to obey their parents. He did it because life works best that way. Children who fail to honor their parents typically grow up to disrespect all authority, making life miserable for everyone.[8]

These biblical principles have at least three points in common with God's natural laws: 1) God authored them; 2) they work consistently; and 3) they are universally applicable to all people in every culture throughout history. And just as the genetic code has not yet been repealed, neither have these dynamic principles.

We know natural laws by observation, but we learn God's spiritual laws by revelation—by reading His Word.

To Our Advantage

It is beyond the scope of this book to cover every principle found in the Bible. But seeing how these thirteen operate can help us identify other principles as we encounter them in Scripture.

These principles are part of a beautifully designed system. The more we understand and work God's system, the better off we are—both in this life and in the life to come. All the principles in this book are designed in such a way that how we respond to them determines our outcome. Happiness comes our way when we live in harmony with His arrangements. But if we try to buck the system God designed for our ultimate well-being, then we will discover, to our eternal sorrow, that He meant exactly what He said. As Carroll B. Ellis put it, ". . . when you go against the grain of the universe you get splinters in your soul."[9]

In physics, "Two solid objects cannot occupy the same space at the same time." Referring to this law, someone has commented, "I want it for a bumper sticker. I'm so tired of tailgaters."[10] When we respect this law, we enjoy safer travel. It's vital to understand that God never gives us any arbitrary spiritual laws, but all of His commandments have good reasons behind them, even if we may not always understand what those reasons are.

> So the LORD commanded us to observe all these statutes, to fear the LORD our God **for our good always** and for our survival, as it is today (Deuteronomy 6:24—emphasis added; see 4:40; 5:29, 33; 6:2-3, 18; 10:13; 12:28; Jeremiah 7:23; 32:39).
>
> "Yet you have not listened to Me," declares the LORD, "in order that you might provoke Me to anger with the work of your hands **to your own harm** (Jeremiah 25:7; see 5:25; 7:19).

Although both of these passages relate to the Old Covenant, it is still true that in obeying God, we do so "for our good always." When we disobey, we do so to our own harm. But a word of caution: For us to be convinced that God's way is best, we must give it a fair trial over a long period of time. In the book of Genesis, Joseph had to experience years of unfair treatment before he could fully appreciate that faithfulness eventually does pay off. And if we share the faith of Moses, who kept looking to the reward, we must take eternity into account, living not just for the present but for the long haul. God's principles are at work in our world, even when we cannot see it. Faith believes this! Faith trusts that God is telling us the truth when He makes His promises—even when all appearances are shouting to the contrary, and even though we may wait until this life is over to see their fulfillment (Hebrews 11:8-16).

The principles discussed in this book are God's principles. He authored them and He operates by them. He guarantees them to work. Millions who have gone before us, as well as many living in our day, have given these principles a fair trial and proved them true. But will they work for us? How can we know? Well, there is one way to find out . . . .

CHAPTER 1

Sin's Wages and God's Gift

**For the wages of sin is death, but the free gift of God
is eternal life in Christ Jesus our Lord**

(Romans 6:23)

On December 17, 2009, after thirty-five years behind bars, James Bain walked out a free man. He was released, not because he had served out his time, but because DNA testing proved him innocent. In an imperfect system, some inmates are released who should be incarcerated, and some languish in their cells who should have never been put there in the first place. "To err is human"—and yet with one notable exception, which we'll examine in a moment, God never punishes the innocent. But does He ever release the guilty?

Before Adam and Eve sinned, God had warned them, "From any tree of the garden you may eat freely; but from the tree of the knowledge of good and evil you shall not eat, for in the day that you eat from it you will surely die" (Genesis 2:16-17). Note the word *surely*. The law of sin and death works as surely as the law of gravity. When Eve told Satan what God had said, he countered, "You surely will not die!" (Genesis 3:4). God said "surely." Satan said "surely." Eve then had to decide which "surely" to believe. Both could not be true. Evidently Eve concluded that God had lied.

Obviously, Adam and Eve did not drop dead the day they ate. Philip Yancey observes, ". . . something died inside Adam and Eve that fateful day. Their bodies lived on for many years, but their spirits lost the free and open communion with God."[11] So God wasn't lying.

The Bad News

Today we continue to suffer the consequences of their disobedience. But we cannot attach all the blame on them. In a real sense, all of us fall, as Adam and Eve did. At some point in our youth, we develop the capacity of making conscious, deliberate choices. It is then that God holds us responsible for our choices. Early on, we are faced with temptation. We then decide whether or not to obey God. The first time we choose to disobey, we die spiritually. ". . . all have sinned and fall short of the glory of God . . ." (Romans 3:23). "For the wages of sin is death . . ." (Romans 6:23).

Seeing Sin for What It Is

Each of us has made the same bad bargain our original ancestors made. "All of us like sheep have gone astray, *each of us has turned to his own way* . . ." (Isaiah 53:6, italics added). That's what sin is: choosing my way over God's way, doing what I want instead of what He wants. That's part of what happened in the Garden.

In stark contrast to Adam and Eve's choice is Jesus' prayer in another garden, when He submitted His will to His Father's will at the cost of His life. ". . . not My will, but Yours be done" (Luke 22:42). His choice was the very opposite of Adam and Eve's, but when we sin we are saying to God, in effect, "My will, not Yours, be done." Sin is the expression of self, of ME! Instead of acknowledging God's authority over me by obeying Him, I make myself the supreme authority—thus expelling God from His rightful place in my life.

Sin is putting my desires ahead of the will of my heavenly Father, who made me and who loves me. It is forgetting the One who daily blesses me beyond measure. Sin is selfishness. Sin is ingratitude. Eve used the ears God had created for her and listened to Satan. She used the eyes God designed and gazed at the forbidden fruit. And with the hand God made, she plucked the fruit, brought it to her lips, and gave it to her husband. And then she used her gift of speech to make excuses. But in our own way, don't we do essentially the same thing?

Two Categories of Sin

Because of the state of our heart, we sin in two basic ways: 1) doing what God forbids, as Adam and Eve did in eating the fruit, and 2) failing to do what God said to do. Jesus had some strong words for those who neglect doing what God has directed (Matthew 23:23; 25:41-46; Luke 12:47).

Joe Barnett recalls:

> As a young boy I often heard men pray, "Lord, forgive us our sins of omission and commission." I had no idea of what those words meant. I finally learned. There are things we do that are wrong—sins of commission. And there are things we should do that we neglect—sins of omission. I wouldn't be surprised if our sins of omission are more damaging than our sins of commission. The words we ought to speak for Christ but leave unspoken must deeply grieve him.[12]

A good illustration of sins through commission and omission is found in the parable of the Good Samaritan (Luke 10:30-37). The thugs who attacked the helpless traveler committed robbery and violence. The priest and Levite who passed by the wounded man omitted what the Good Samaritan later provided. Surely these religious leaders knew they should help the roadside victim, yet they did nothing. They did not kick, mock, or curse him—they simply passed him by. Now haven't we all been guilty of both kinds of sin? Haven't we all done what God said not to do, and failed to do what He said to do?

Specific Ways to Sin

Before people are ready to receive God's prescription for sin's remedy, they need to hear His diagnosis.

> Or do you not know that the unrighteous will not inherit the

kingdom of God? Do not be deceived; neither fornicators, nor idolaters, nor adulterers, nor effeminate, nor homosexuals, nor thieves, nor the covetous, nor drunkards, nor revilers, nor swindlers, will inherit the kingdom of God (1 Corinthians 6:9-10)

Now the deeds of the flesh are evident, which are: immorality, impurity, sensuality, idolatry, sorcery, enmities, strife, jealousy, outbursts of anger, disputes, dissensions, factions, envying, drunkenness, carousing, and things like these, of which I forewarn you, just as I have forewarned you, that those who practice such things will not inherit the kingdom of God (Galatians 5:19-21).

But for the cowardly and unbelieving and abominable and murderers and immoral persons and sorcerers and idolaters and all liars, their part will be in the lake that burns with fire and brimstone, which is the second death (Revelation 21:8).

These three lists demonstrate just how many different ways there are to sin—and other passages refer to even more sins than those listed above. Do you find some of your sins on these lists, as I do?

Accepting the Diagnosis

Such lists are designed to expose our guilt before a holy God so that we will then be open to the good news of God's grace. We must own up to the bad news of our fatal condition before we see our need for a cure. We can't be converted unless we are first convicted.

We often say, "God hates the sin but loves the sinner." This is blessedly true, but too often we quickly rush over the first half of this statement to get to the second. We cannot escape the fact that God hates our sins. We may trifle with our sins or excuse them, but God hates them.[13]

Sin is far worse than we might imagine. It pains God deeply to see what we do to ourselves when we sin. He also abhors the harm we do to others. And He detests what sin does to our relationship with Him. He created us to have fellowship with Him.

He yearns for our friendship. But sin erects a barrier between us. Even though we're the ones who have built that wall, brick by brick, sin by sin, there is no way we can remove it on our own. The wall remains—and grows thicker and higher by the day—until we give Him our consent to take it down. No wonder God hates sin so much!

Have we really come to grips with the gravity of sin? It has been well said, "Nothing so blinds us to the real character of sin as the fact that it is our own." [14] Alexander Maclaren pulls no punches:

> . . . if we were turned inside out, and every foul, creeping thing, and every blotch and spot upon these hearts of ours spread in the light, we could not face one another; we could scarcely face ourselves. [15]

> If you have never been down on your knees before God, feeling what a wicked man or woman you are, I doubt hugely whether you will ever stand with radiant face before God, and praise Him through eternity for His mercy to you. [16]

The Bible warns us about refusing to acknowledge sin:

> There is a kind who is pure in his own eyes,
> Yet is not washed from his filthiness" (Proverbs 30:12).

> This is the way of an adulterous woman:
> She eats and wipes her mouth,
> And says, "I have done no wrong" (Proverbs 30:20).

> Were they ashamed because of the abomination they have done?
> They were not even ashamed at all;
> They did not even know how to blush (Jeremiah 6:15).

> If we say that we have no sin, we are deceiving ourselves and the truth is not in us . . . . If we say that we have not sinned, we make Him a liar and His word is not in us (1 John 1:8, 10).

But not everyone is willing to accept God's verdict of "Guilty!" Wayne W. Dyer boldly asserts, "You are sinning only if you believe you are, and each person in the world can judge 'sin' in any way he chooses."[17] *Oh, really?!* Does God have no say in the matter?

Isn't He the one who determines what is right and wrong, good and evil? To deny personal sin, John says, is to call God a liar.

Perhaps the three most difficult words we could ever say are: "I have sinned." Just saying the words, of course, doesn't get the job done, but we must sincerely, deeply mean them—and then take God's prescription for the cure. King Saul said the right words, "I have sinned" when confronted by Samuel for his disobedience (1 Samuel 15:24), but his confession was practically wrung out of him. On a later occasion he admitted, "I have sinned," showing apparently genuine remorse for his murderous pursuit of David (1 Samuel 26:21), but his subsequent actions showed no evidence of what, centuries later, John the Baptist would demand: ". . . bear fruit in keeping with repentance"—a changed life (Matthew 3:8; see Luke 3:8-14; Acts 26:20). In addition, there were others in the Bible who said, "I have sinned," but there was no apparent change in their attitude or behavior (Exodus 9:27; Numbers 14:40; 22:34). In contrast, when David admitted, "I have sinned" (2 Samuel 12:13; 24:10), his confession rang true (Psalm 51). He was genuinely penitent and God forgave him.

Tommy South explains,

> What God is looking for is an openness, a transparency within us that attempts to hide nothing from Him, but simply confesses what we are and what we have done, so that we can be cleansed by Jesus' blood. When we confess our sins, we aren't giving God any new information. He already knows exactly who we are and exactly what we have done. When we say, "I have sinned," we are showing a spirit of humility and of seeking after Him.[18]

What Sin Does to Us

"For the wages of sin is death . . ." (Romans 6:23a). In view of the eternal consequences, why do we choose to sin? James Burton Coffman writes:

> Such unsatisfactory wages of sin, it seems, should make sin

a very unprofitable employer, and long ago have resulte
the cessation of all sin; but not so. True, if the full accoui...
sin's wages should be posted and paid at the end of every day,
there would doubtless be far less sinning. It is the "buy now,
pay later" aspect of the penalty of sin which commends it as
an attractive employment for many; but this verse is a warning
that payment is certain, and that "death" is the *quid pro quo* of
sin. "This for that!"[19]

Two verses earlier, Paul had asked, "Therefore what benefit
were you then deriving from the things of which you are now
ashamed? For the outcome of those things is death" (Romans
6:21). James describes the whole sordid process from start to
finish:

Let no one say when he is tempted, "I am being tempted by
God"; for God cannot be tempted by evil, and He Himself does
not tempt anyone. But each one is tempted when he is carried
away and enticed by his own lust. Then when lust has conceived,
it gives birth to sin; and when sin is accomplished, it brings forth
death (James 1:13-15).

In other words: temptation → lust → sin → death. A good
illustration of this fatal progression is found in the story of
Achan who disobeyed God's order not to take any of the spoils
of battle from the city of Jericho. When confronted with his sin,
he admitted:

Truly, I have sinned against the LORD, the God of Israel, and this
is what I did: when I saw among the spoil a beautiful mantle
from Shinar and two hundred shekels of silver and a bar of gold
fifty shekels in weight, then I coveted them and took them; and
behold, they are concealed in the earth inside my tent with the
silver underneath it (Joshua 7:20-21).

Seeing the valuables, he was tempted. He coveted (lusted for)
them. He took them. And for this he was stoned. But why, oh
why, did he do it? Phillip D. O'Hern explains:

Myopia—it means nearsightedness . . . . Achan was spiritually nearsighted. He saw only the treasures in front of him that he wanted so badly. He did not see God's plan for the Israelite nation. He did not see the battles that were yet to be won. He did not see the land of milk and honey awaiting their victories.

Because he did not see God's plans, because he chose to take care of himself instead of letting God take care of him, he was killed. What a price to pay for nearsightedness![20]

If Achan had it to do over again, would he think it was still worth it? Would he believe his hidden stash was worth Israel's humiliating defeat in the battle with Ai, including the loss of some thirty-six men, as a direct consequence of his selfishness? He died knowing that he had troubled Israel (Joshua 22:20). He died knowing he had angered God. He died knowing that he had exchanged his own life, the lives of his children, and his reputation for mere things.

Is sin ever worth the high price tag it carries? Evidently Achan thought he could get away with hiding the loot under his tent. Apparently he failed to take God into account. Even if we successfully escape detection from our fellows, who can hide from God? ". . . be sure your sin will find you out" (Numbers 32:23). Unless we take God's antidote for sin's penalty, we will experience what the book of Revelation calls the second death—hell (Revelation 20:14; 21:8). "For the wages of sin is death . . . ." Sin does not pay minimum wage. As Cecil May III says, "Two thousand years later sin still eternally condemns. There is no inflation or deflation in this wage. The end consequence of sin remains unchanged."[21] And every person in sin's prison is on death row.

The Good News
So the Bad News is death—alienation from the Author of life followed by eternal death in hell—this is sin's ultimate consequence. This is an expression of God's justice. Since He

has condemned sin, and since He declared death to be its wages, how can He be a just God if He fails to punish?

But God is not only just, He is also merciful. If it weren't for His mercy, would we have any hope? "'The person who sins will die'. . . . 'For why will you die, O house of Israel? For I have no pleasure in the death of anyone who dies,' declares the Lord GOD. 'Therefore, repent and live'" (Ezekiel 18:20, 31b-32). "The Lord is . . . patient toward you, not wishing for any to perish but for all to come to repentance" (2 Peter 3:9). God "desires all men to be saved and to come to the knowledge of the truth" (1 Timothy 2:4). But how can God be both just and merciful at the same time? Is there a resolution to the tension between God's justice and His mercy? Can God Himself resolve this apparent impasse?

The Solution

Our sin problem is resolved in Christ and only in Him. First, He is without sin (Hebrews 4:15). If He had sinned—even once—He would be in the same sad predicament with all the rest of us. He could do nothing for us.

The animal sacrifices offered during the old Mosaic covenant had to be without blemish to be acceptable to God. This requirement was a "preview" of the One whom John the Baptist hailed as "the Lamb of God who takes away the sin of the world!" (John 1:29). Peter says that we are redeemed "with precious blood, as of a lamb unblemished and spotless, the blood of Christ" (1 Peter 1:19).

Second, God "made Him who knew no sin to be sin on our behalf, so that we might become the righteousness of God in Him" (2 Corinthians 5:21). The Innocent One was treated as if He were guilty. Here is the sole exception to the rule that God never punishes the innocent. Ironically, the only ONE who ever kept God's law perfectly was executed as a criminal between two thieves. This makes it possible for us to become God's righteousness in Christ. Has there ever been a more dramatic role reversal?

". . . He Himself bore our sins in His body on the cross, so that we might die to sin and live to righteousness; for by His wounds you were healed" (1 Peter 2:24). These words echo the greatest Old Testament prophecy of Christ, recorded seven centuries before its fulfillment:

> Surely our griefs He Himself bore,
> And our sorrows He carried;
> Yet we ourselves esteemed Him stricken,
> Smitten of God, and afflicted.
> But He was pierced through for our transgressions,
> He was crushed for our iniquities;
> The chastening for our well-being fell upon Him,
> And by His scourging we are healed.
> All of us like sheep have gone astray,
> Each of us has turned to his own way;
> But the LORD has caused the iniquity of us all
> To fall on Him (Isaiah 53:4-6).

What theologians call the substitutionary atonement of Christ simply means that Jesus took the full brunt of the punishment we deserve. We were alienated from our holy God because of our sin, but Christ's death makes it possible for us to be reconciled to God.

> For **while we were still helpless**, at the right time Christ died for the ungodly. For one will hardly die for a righteous man; though perhaps for the good man someone would dare even to die. But God demonstrates His own love toward us, in that **while we were yet sinners**, Christ died for us. Much more then, having now been justified by His blood, we shall be saved from the wrath of God through Him. For if **while we were enemies** we were reconciled to God through the death of His Son, much more, having been reconciled, we shall be saved by His life. And not only this, but we also exult in God through our Lord Jesus Christ, through whom we have now received the reconciliation (Romans 5:6-11, emphasis added).

Our Alienated Condition	What Reconciliation Cost	What Reconciliation Does
While we were still helpless	Christ **died** for the ungodly.	
While we were yet sinners	God demonstrates His own love toward us in that Christ **died** for us.	Having now been justified by His blood, we shall be **saved from the wrath of God** through Him.
While we were enemies	We were reconciled to God through the **death** of His Son.	Having been reconciled [to God], we shall be **saved by His life**. We also exult in God through our Lord Jesus Christ, through whom we have now received the reconciliation.

Helpless, ungodly sinners—enemies! Are we willing to accept this extremely unflattering portrait of our alienated, unredeemed condition? Unless and until we do acknowledge this painfully accurate diagnosis, we are not ready for God's cure. We must face the bad news before we can receive the good news.

So what's the good news? The good news is: God punished His Son (who didn't deserve it), instead of us (who do deserve it). Jesus died so we won't have to. As the middle column of the chart above makes clear, His death is the key to our salvation. No higher price has ever been paid for anything! As the third column above shows, we are justified (made right) and reconciled to our holy God who hates sin. As Charles B. Hodge Jr. says, "The same God who poured His wrath out on Christ at the cross will pour that same wrath out at judgment. God is the same God at the cross and at judgment. Either Jesus is punished for my sins or I am!" [22]

Both Jesus and we are undeserving. He didn't deserve death. We don't deserve life. What we don't deserve is offered us as a gift. So at the cross both God's justice and His mercy are satisfied. He punished sin because He is just. He extended grace as an expression of His mercy. Who would have ever thought of such an arrangement? And even if someone could have imagined such a thing, who but God could make it happen?

This is amazing enough, but even more astounding is that both the Father and the Son were actually willing to go through with it. "For God so loved the world, that He gave His only begotten Son . . ." (John 3:16). "We know love by this, that He laid down His life for us . . ." (1 John 3:16). "Greater love has no one than this, that one lay down his life for his friends" (John 15:13).

Imagine someone climbing aboard a bloodmobile and announcing, "Now listen, before I donate, I want you to assure me that my blood will go only to someone who deserves it." The greatest Blood Donor in human history made no such demand. No one who benefits from His blood deserves it, which is, of course, why He gave His blood in the first place.

The Greatest Gift

G. C. Brewer put his finger on the problem for a lot of folks: "If we were called upon to name . . . the one thing that the present day world needs more than anything else, we should say, a sense of sin." [23] If we are willing to face up to the bad-news half of Romans 6:23 ("For the wages of sin is death . . . ."), then we are ready to proceed to the good news: ". . . but the free gift of God is eternal life in Christ Jesus our Lord." Thank God for the last half of Romans 6:23! Imagine if all we had were those first dreadful seven words—"For the wages of sin is death"—Period. But instead, the bad news—death—is completely cancelled out by the good news—eternal life.

Is God obligated to save us? Wouldn't He still be a just God if

He let us all die in our sins? Isn't that what we truly deserve? But God's great loving heart won't let Him leave us on death row. "For the law of the Spirit of life in Christ Jesus has set you free from **the law of sin and of death**" (Romans 8:2, emphasis added). ". . . everyone who commits sin is **the slave of sin** . . . . So if the Son makes you free, you will be free indeed" (John 8:34, 36).

James Bain was released after doing time—a long time—for someone else's crime. We too can be freed, but not because we are innocent. Far from it. And yet our record of offenses, no matter how many, no matter how heinous, can be wiped off our record once and for all. But how?

How We Respond to Such Love

When Jesus prayed on the cross, "Father, forgive them; for they do not know what they are doing" (Luke 23:34), did God immediately grant forgiveness to everyone? About seven weeks after Jesus died, Peter stood up on the great day of Pentecost and preached the first gospel sermon following Jesus' return to heaven. When he convicted his hearers of having killed their Messiah, they cried out in anguish, "Brethren, what shall we do?" (Acts 2:37). How did Peter answer? Did he say, "There's nothing you can do. You had your chance, and you blew it! God sent you the Messiah, and you murdered Him. There is nothing for you but hell"? Or on the opposite extreme did he say, "There's nothing you can do. Christ did it all. Just believe!"? And did Peter tell them, "Confess that you are a sinner in need of grace; ask Jesus into Your heart; receive Him as your personal Savior"—and then lead them in saying the "sinner's prayer"?

In answer to the question, "Brethren, what shall we do?" here's what Peter actually did say: "Repent, and each of you be baptized in the name of Jesus Christ for the forgiveness of your sins; and you will receive the gift of the Holy Spirit" (Acts 2:38). A few verses later the text says, "So then, those who had received his word were baptized; and that day there were added about three thousand souls" (v. 41). A few more verses later it says, "And the Lord was adding to their number day by day those who were being saved" (v. 47).

Who were added by the Lord to their number? Those who were being saved. How were they added? They received the word and were baptized. And what did those who were baptized experience? God's forgiveness and the gift of the Spirit! *That's grace!*

On the cross Jesus had prayed, "Father, forgive them . . . ." Now they were! To this day, Jesus' prayer continues to be answered whenever we respond as did the three thousand. When we do what they did, God releases us from death row and sets us free.

Baptism is faith expressed in penitence and obedience (Mark 16:16; Acts 2:38; 22:16; Galatians 3:26-27; 1 Peter 3:21). It is at the very moment of our baptism that we make that vital connection with Jesus' death and resurrection (Colossians 2:12-13), and all our sins are washed away (Acts 22:16). Baptism is a reenactment of Jesus' burial and resurrection (Romans 6:3-5). But it is not a mere symbol of these central events; rather, it is faith obeying. As James Denney said, ". . . baptism and faith are but the outside and the inside of the same thing." [24] It is a dramatic moment of grace granted and grace received. God provides us with baptism so we can "plug into" the dynamic saving power of the cross and empty tomb.

And Then . . . ?

Once we take that initial step of faith, what then? Jude urges Christians, ". . . keep yourselves in the love of God, waiting anxiously for the mercy of our Lord Jesus Christ to eternal life" (Jude 21). Peter exhorts, ". . . be all the more diligent to make certain about His calling and choosing you; for as long as you practice these things, you will never stumble . . ." (2 Peter 1:10). Paul offers both a warning and a promise: ". . . for if you are living according to the flesh, you must die; but if by the Spirit you are putting to death the deeds of the body, you will live" (Romans 8:13).

What could be sadder than a Christian who falls away from Christ? In such cases a rescue operation is desperately needed, and here's where fellow believers can help. As James says, "My brethren, if any among you strays from the truth and one turns him back, let him know that he who turns a sinner from the error of his way will save his soul from death and will cover a multitude of sins" (James 5:19-20). The expression "any among you" obviously refers to those who had been saved, but then strayed (see 1 Timothy 5:5-6; 2 Peter 2:20-22). Here "death" cannot mean the death of the body (the first death). Even the saved are mortal—the body must die (Hebrews 9:27). But as Jesus said to one of His churches, "He who overcomes will not be hurt by the second death" (Revelation 2:11). The second death is hell (Revelation 21:8). Thank God, we have to die only once!

Once is enough.

Questions:

1. Read Romans 6:21a. What "benefit" do sinners think they are getting from their lifestyle?
2. Read Proverbs 30:20 and Jeremiah 6:15. Why do some feel no apparent sense of guilt?
3. Why does God take sin so much more seriously than we do?
4. How much did sin cost God?
5. How much does sin cost us?
6. How does the "long view" help us to have the right perspective on sin's wages and God's gift?

CHAPTER 2

Choose Your Master

**No one can serve two masters . . . .
You cannot serve God and wealth**

(Matthew 6:24)

One Saturday evening after buying gas to do some mowing, I gave the attendant $20 and received $17 in change. Not having my wallet, I stuffed the money into my pocket.

Later while mowing, I repeatedly picked up litter off the lawn and stuffed it into my pocket. Twice, I emptied my pocket into the trash container in the garage. Later that evening I suddenly remembered the $17. (You're way ahead of me, aren't you?) Sure enough, there they were: a ten, a five, and two ones crumpled up among the litter.

Cash and trash. That which had value was mixed in with what was worse than worthless. Cash can be exchanged for bread and milk, air conditioning and electricity, tuition and books. But how much can you do with trash?

Any day in America, millions of hard-earned bucks are thrown away on the lottery or other gambling ventures. Earnings are exchanged for addictive substances that harm the wonderful human body God made for us. Money is traded for what corrupts the soul: porn, illicit entertainment, and sex for hire. Cash for trash.

On the other hand, money is traded for greeting cards and postage to send notes to those who are hurting or lonely. Money is used to buy Bibles for prisoners or for people in other countries who don't have their own copy. Dollars buy food for people displaced by war or natural disasters. Donations finance medical research, build hospitals, endow foundations—and most importantly, support the preaching of the gospel.

Is money good or evil? Certainly, it can do great good or great harm. But how we think of it is even more important than how we use it. Our challenge is to make and use money without letting it take over. In the parable of the sower, Jesus said that the ground infested with thorns represents the person "who hears the word, and the worry of the world and the deceitfulness of wealth choke the word, and it becomes unfruitful" (Matthew 13:22). Of the various hindrances to fruitful discipleship cited by Jesus in interpreting this parable (Matthew 13:18-23), could this be the one to which affluent American Christians are most vulnerable? Paul says that "those who want to get rich fall into temptation and a snare and many foolish and harmful desires which plunge men into ruin and destruction," and that "some by longing for [money] have wandered away from the faith and pierced themselves with many griefs" (1 Timothy 6:9, 10).

What Are Our Options?

Our verse in the King James Version reads, "Ye cannot serve God and mammon." "Mammon" is the transliteration of the Aramaic *mammōnas* and is defined as "wealth in all its forms"[25] and "material possessions."[26] It is rendered "mammon" in some versions and translated as "wealth" or "money" in others. Some versions capitalize the word as "Mammon" to show that Jesus is personifying it as a god that is worshiped. R. A. Torrey asks, "What is an idol? An idol is anything that takes the place of God, anything that is the supreme object of our affection. God alone has the right to the supreme place in our hearts. Everything and everyone else must be subordinate to Him."[27] Since money can so easily take first place in the human heart, thus supplanting God, it is no wonder that Paul equates greed with idolatry (Colossians 3:5; see Ephesians 5:5).

Is mammon inherently evil? What Paul condemns as "a root of all sorts of evil" is not money *per se* but the love of money

(1 Timothy 6:10). The real issue is: What is our attitude toward money? If we look at it simply as a commodity to be gratefully received and responsibly used to God's glory, then it is not our god, and we do not serve it. But how easily mammon morphs into our master when we love it and give it top priority. As N. Lamar Reinsch Jr. says, "A materialist is someone who values too highly the artifacts and experiences of this life. Materialism is not a lifestyle. It is an attitude . . . . There are two realities: a physical one and a spiritual one. The physical reality is beautiful and good—but subordinate to the spiritual reality. A materialist is simply someone with his priorities upside down." [28]

How we think of money makes all the difference. For example, the bronze serpent that God commanded Moses to construct (Numbers 21:6-9) was nothing more than a metallic object with no inherent powers. When the snake-bitten Israelites looked at it, they were healed, but their healing came from God, not from the bronze serpent. Looking at the serpent was simply the condition God required for Israel to demonstrate obedient faith toward Him. But centuries later, some began worshiping it as a god. As a result, King Hezekiah had to destroy it (2 Kings 18:4). What had changed? The change was not in the molecular makeup of the bronze serpent nor in its shape or appearance. Rather, the change took place in the mind of the viewers. Likewise with money. Our view of it either keeps it in its proper place as a useful resource or it "materializes" into God's rival. Our Father loves us too much to tolerate competitors for our affection toward Him. It hurts Him deeply when we receive His gifts and then turn our attention from Him to them.

It's impressive how much Jesus had to say about materialism. Could it be He knew we just might have a problem with greed? "You cannot serve God and wealth." When we study this principle in its context in the Sermon on the Mount, we find it sandwiched between two sections on how we should and should not feel about material things.

The First Error

In verses Matthew 6:19-21 Jesus warns,

> Do not store up for yourselves treasures on earth, where moth and rust destroy, and where thieves break in and steal. But store up for yourselves treasures in heaven, where neither moth nor rust destroys, and where thieves do not break in or steal; for where your treasure is, there your heart will be also.

Foy E. Wallace offers a needed clarification:

> This precept is not a prohibition against provision for temporal security. Such an injunction would contradict the apostolic reference to the parental obligation of 2 Corinthians 12:14: "For the children ought not to lay up for the parents, but the parents for the children." The . . . form of speech that denied the lesser in order to emphasize the greater is often employed in the New Testament. An example of it is evident in a similar statement by the Lord in John 6:27: "Labour not for the meat which perisheth, but for that meat which endureth unto eternal life." The Lord did not forbid working for a living, for his apostle said in 2 Thessalonians 3:10, "This we command you, that if any would not work, neither should he eat." In a negative form of speech the lesser was denied that the greater might be more emphatically affirmed.[29]

"Your treasure," says Ron Blue, "is the thing that is most important to you. Maybe it's a job promotion, a new house, or a new car . . . . Regardless of your particular passion, your treasure is what you think about, what you go after, what you want to attain. It's where your heart is."[30] When we say, "My heart's not in it," what do we mean? When Jesus said, ". . . where your treasure is, there your heart will be also," isn't He wanting us to examine where our heart is—and isn't? Either we are heaven-oriented or earthbound.

When Our Treasures Leave Us

The problem with earthly treasures, Jesus says, is their susceptibility to loss. Even unbelievers acknowledge that their "stuff" is vulnerable. Though some 2,000 years have passed since Jesus said this, we are still fighting moths/rust/thieves. These three are representative of a much longer list of treasure-busters, including:

tornadoes/earthquakes/tsunamis/hurricanes/floods
landslides/erosion/drought/hail/lightning/fire
mold/termites/dry rot/wear-and-tear
corrosion/breakage/inflation
recession/bear markets
computer viruses
identify theft
vandalism
terrorism
wars
etc.

Do not weary yourself to gain wealth,
Cease from your consideration of it.
When you set your eyes on it, it is gone.
For wealth certainly makes itself wings
Like an eagle that flies toward the heavens.
(Proverbs 23:4-5)

To a grocer, perishables include items with a short shelf life, such as produce, meats, dairy products, etc. To Jesus, not only is everything in the store perishable, but even the store building itself. During the time we've lived in our town, two grocery stores have burned to the ground. Even gold and silver, Peter says, are perishable (1 Peter 1:7, 18). One of these days all the gold in Fort Knox will experience total meltdown (2 Peter 3:10-12).

People in the investment world speak of "securities." Is anything material really secure? There is no 100 percent safe investment except for what Jesus recommends—laying up treasure in heaven—untouched by all those earthly risks that can so easily separate us from our stuff. Although Jesus doesn't explain here how we lay up treasure in heaven, other passages make it clear that we do it by sharing with those in need (Matthew 19:21; Luke 12:33-34; 1 Timothy 6:17-19).

In a remarkable passage, the writer of Hebrews reminds his readers of something that happened to them not long after their conversion:

> But remember the former days, when, after being enlightened, you endured a great conflict of sufferings, partly by being made a public spectacle through reproaches and tribulations, and partly by becoming sharers with those who were so treated. For you showed sympathy to the prisoners and **accepted joyfully the seizure of your property, knowing that you have for yourselves a better possession and a lasting one.** Therefore, do not throw away your confidence, which has a great reward (Hebrews 10:32-35, emphasis added).

What impresses me is their attitude toward the loss of their possessions. Focused on what they had to gain, they could rejoice in spite of what they lost. Financial loss to them didn't really matter! They were focused on the future, not the here-and-now. I can't help but wonder if I could rejoice as they did. Could you?

When We Leave Our Treasures

But what if we take every precaution to guard our possessions against loss? We install a state-of-the-art security system. We purchase comprehensive homeowners and auto insurance. We develop a diversified portfolio and make sure we have an inflation hedge in place. The irony of life, however, is that even if we could somehow successfully beat all the treasure-busters and never lose a penny, we must someday leave everything we own to others. As James wrote, ". . . the rich man in the midst of his pursuits will fade away" (James 1:11). This is what the prosperous farmer in Jesus' parable failed to take into account. (How easy it is to do!) His stated goal was to retire and take it easy. By American standards he was a successful man. He was a planner with big ideas for expansion:

And he began reasoning to himself, saying, "What shall I do, since I have no place to store my crops?" Then he said, "This is what I will do: I will tear down my barns and build larger ones, and there I will store all my grain and my goods. And I will say to my soul, 'Soul, you have many goods laid up for many years to come; take your ease, eat, drink and be merry'" (Luke 12:17-19).

"What shall I do . . . ?" Is there anything wrong with his question? It expresses a perfectly legitimate concern. He had to do something with his surplus. But what? His question is one we must all ask ourselves as we manage our financial resources. "What shall I do with what I own?" It's the right question, but apparently he asked it for the wrong reasons, so he gave it the wrong answer. Note what he did not say: "How thankful I am to God for all these blessings! What a huge responsibility I have to be a good steward of what God has so graciously given me! How can I bless others with all this abundance?"

Many readers have noticed how often "I" and "my" appear in his little speech. It's all about ME! He had nothing to say about God and nothing about others. All he could talk about was his own future and his own pleasure. He had a two-phase plan for his wealth: first, store it up; then, live it up. He kept saying, "I will . . . . I will . . . . I will . . . ." But God said to him, in effect: "Oh no, you won't!" He told him:

"You fool! This very night your soul is required of you; and now who will own what you have prepared?" So is the man who stores up treasure for himself, and is not rich toward God.

He bet everything on having "many goods laid up for many years to come." Many goods for many years. Instead, his time ran out, he left everything behind, and he forfeited his soul. He gambled and he lost . . . *big time!* Hardly a story with a happy ending. But it didn't have to end this way. It never does.

Wealth: Its Lures and Limitations

What's interesting about the story Jesus told of the rich farmer is His reason for telling it:

> Someone in the crowd said to Him, "Teacher, tell my brother to divide the family inheritance with me." But He said to him, "Man, who appointed Me a judge or arbitrator over you?" Then He said to them, "Beware, and be on your guard against every form of greed; for not even when one has an abundance does his life consist of his possessions." And He told them a parable, saying, "The land of a rich man was very productive . . ." (Luke 12:13-16).

From the perspective of the man who wanted Jesus to confront his brother, the most important words in his statement were not *Teacher* or *my brother*, but rather, *inheritance* and *me*.

After my mother died, we had an estate sale. The auctioneer who handled the sale told me he had seen family members divide over who would get a particular item that had once belonged to a deceased parent. He said he had been materialistic, but after being in this business, he now feels he owns nothing he couldn't part with if need be.

The man who said, "Teacher, tell my brother to divide the family inheritance with me," and the rich farmer in Jesus' parable both fell prey to what Jesus calls "the deceitfulness of wealth" (Matthew 13:22). Wealth deceives us . . .

>   . . . if it gives us a false sense of security

>   . . . when it becomes the master, making us its slaves while allowing us to think we're still in charge

>   . . . if we let it distract us from our ultimate purpose

>   . . . if we allow it to warp our values and skew our priorities

>   . . . if God is banished from our thinking

>   . . . if it makes us feel self-sufficient and blinds us to the needs of those around us

. . . if we think we would be happy if we just had more.

Mammon is a master of deception. The only way any of us can avoid being deceived by it is: a) knowing how deceitful it can be, and b) shaping our values according to Christ, not according to the world.

A Second Error

Immediately following Jesus' warning about the impossibility of serving both God and mammon is a lengthy section on trusting our Father to provide for our daily needs instead of anxiously pursuing those needs as if God had no part in the equation (Matthew 6:25-34). The most important verse in this passage is the one in which Jesus says, "But seek first His kingdom and His righteousness, and all these things [food and clothing] will be added to you." Giving priority to bodily needs comes so naturally, almost instinctively, but faith requires putting spiritual concerns ahead of physical. Jesus guarantees that our heavenly Father will take care of us if we show we believe this promise. Do we really? "Worry," says William Barclay, "is essentially distrust of God."[31]

If we fail to trust Him as our Provider, we will continue to run scared. We will be consumed by our own getting-and-keeping. We will end up like the rich fool in Jesus' parable. Instead of being consumers, we become the consumed. And it's all so unnecessary.

Zig Ziglar said it well:

> . . . many people have complete faith in the incredible and very little faith in the simple day-to-day promises our Lord makes. Many Christians have no trouble with, "In the beginning God created the Heavens and the Earth." Or, "Go thy way: thy faith hath made thee whole" (Mark 10:52). They have no trouble believing He parted the waters of the Red Sea so that approximately three million Jews could walk through. They have no trouble believing that Christ walked on water, arose from the dead, or fed the multitudes. They have no trouble believing the big things, but "You see, Lord, I've got this car payment, it's due

next Thursday, and it is nearly two hundred dollars. Let's face it, Lord, You might can split water, but you've never dealt with a finance company before." [32]

Our Challenge

G. Campbell Morgan comments on the sections preceding and following our key text: ". . . He warned His disciples and all the subjects of His kingdom against two perils, those of covetousness and of care; the desire to possess and the anxiety lest not enough may be possessed to meet the bare necessities of life." [33]

These two wrong attitudes—desiring earthly treasures and worrying about daily necessities—are different forms of granting mammon the place that only God deserves. Money becomes the focus, not God. Eldred Echols said it well: "The Christian is given the high calling of using money without serving money." [34]

Why So Much Emphasis?

Sometimes Jesus repeated lessons. Luke records another occasion where He taught on the right and wrong uses of money and restated the principle, "You cannot serve God and wealth" (Luke 16:13). It's noteworthy that the next verse says, "Now the Pharisees, who were lovers of money, were listening to all these things and were scoffing at Him." As Frank L. Cox says, "No one scoffs at a scriptural lesson on giving but the lover of money." [35]

In a congregation where I served as preacher, the elders asked me to preach on giving once every three months. It was a challenge, to say the least, to keep coming up with fresh ways of approaching this vital topic. Years ago, at the request of an elder, I preached on giving four Sundays in a row. Then I found this unsigned note in the sermon suggestion box: "Enough about giving. Let's have sermons about keeping our souls." Revealing comment!—especially in view of the fact that a major factor in "keeping our souls" is the right attitude toward material things.

The rich farmer of Jesus' parable, referred to above, needed to hear some pointed lessons on giving, and so did another rich man we'll be examining in the next section. Both failed to keep their souls because they had let their wealth become their god. What happened to them can happen to us. Richard J. Foster makes a needed point: "Giving has a way of routing out the tough old miser within us. Even the poor need to know that they can give. Just the very act of letting go of money, or some other treasure, does something within us. It destroys the demon greed."[36]

"Enough about giving"? Hardly! If we are to overcome our natural tendency toward materialism, and develop instead the generous spirit God wants in us, we need more than an occasional reminder. We need the renewing of our mind (Romans 12:2; Ephesians 4:22-24). We need an overhaul of our priorities. We need the mind of Christ (Philippians 2:5). Jesus was no materialist. Once someone said to Jesus, "I will follow You wherever You go." Jesus replied, "The foxes have holes and the birds of the air have nests, but the Son of Man has nowhere to lay His head" (Luke 9:57-58). "For you know the grace of our Lord Jesus Christ, that though He was rich, yet for your sake He became poor, so that you through His poverty might become rich" (2 Corinthians 8:9).

The Bankrupt Rich Man

Luke 16 ends with the story of the rich man and Lazarus. This rich man indulged himself in a luxurious lifestyle. He had more than plenty—until he died. Then he had nothing but unrelieved agony and fear that his five brothers would end up where he was. Not only did he leave all he had behind, but there was no treasure in heaven waiting for him. The rich man could have laid up for himself heavenly treasure by helping Lazarus, lying helpless at his gate. But now it was too late to help Lazarus and too late to repent of his selfishness. In torment this former rich man discovered how totally bankrupt he was.

Will we learn from his short-sightedness? Earlier we considered Jesus' warning, "Beware, and be on your guard against every form of greed; for not even when one has an abundance does his life consist of his possessions" (Luke 12:15). Ever since Jesus said that, people have been trying to prove Him wrong. The cry of our culture is: Have! Get! Keep! More! Yet everyone wants to go to heaven. Perhaps you've heard about the boy who announced after hearing the story of the rich man and Lazarus, "I want to be the rich man while I'm living, but Lazarus after I die!"

"You Cannot Serve God and Wealth"

Passage	Earthly Priorities	Heavenly Priorities
Matthew 6:31-33	Do not worry then, saying, "What will we eat?" or "What will we drink?" or "What will we wear for clothing?" For the Gentiles eagerly seek all these things	But seek first His kingdom and His righteousness, and all these things will be added to you.
Mark 10:21-22, 29-30	Looking at him, Jesus felt a love for him and said to him, "One thing you lack: go and sell all you possess and give to the poor, and you will have treasure in heaven; and come, follow Me." But at these words he was saddened, and he went away grieving, for he was one who owned much property.	Truly I say to you, there is no one who has left house or brothers or sisters or mother or father or children or farms, for My sake and for the gospel's sake, but that he will receive a hundred times as much now in the present age, houses and brothers and sisters and mothers and children and farms, along with persecutions; and in the age to come, eternal life.

Passage	Earthly Priorities	Heavenly Priorities
1 Timothy 6:9-11	But those who want to get rich fall into temptation and a snare and many foolish and harmful desires which plunge men into ruin and destruction. For the love of money is a root of all sorts of evil, and some by longing for it have wandered away from the faith and pierced themselves with many griefs.	But flee from these things, you man of God, and pursue righteousness, godliness, faith, love, perseverance and gentleness.
1 Timothy 6:17-19	Instruct those who are rich in this present world not to be conceited or to fix their hope on the uncertainty of riches,	but on God, who richly supplies us with all things to enjoy. Instruct them to do good, to be rich in good works, to be generous and ready to share, storing up for themselves the treasure of a good foundation for the future, so that they may take hold of that which is life indeed.

The Blessedness of a United Heart

One thing is clear: God will not tolerate rivals. He deserves and demands exclusive rights over us, our undivided attention, our single-minded devotion. ". . . for you shall not worship any other god, for the LORD, whose name is Jealous, is a jealous God . . ." (Exodus 34:14; see 20:2-5).

Like the rich young ruler, too many Christians want eternal life but are pulled away by the Mammon Magnet. Israel tried to serve both God and idols (2 Kings 17:33, 41; Zephaniah 1:4-5). It didn't work then; it won't work now; it never will work. "No one can serve two masters . . . ." Why not? ". . . for either he will hate the one and love the other, or he will be devoted to one and despise the other. You cannot serve God and wealth." Cannot means cannot. "You shall love the Lord your God with *all* your heart and with *all* your soul and with *all* your might" (Deuteronomy 6:5, italics added). Giving lip service to spiritual values while living for the here-and-now results in what is called "cognitive dissonance." *Cognitive* refers to what we know; *dissonance* means discord, disharmony. Our mind tells us how we ought to be, but our lifestyle is pulling us in the opposite direction. We simply can't handle the inner conflict created by competing loyalties. God designed us to focus on one thing.

A united heart, one that is totally in tune with the will of God, is a heart at peace. A distracted disciple will be a defeated disciple if he doesn't wake up and regain his focus. As D. A. Carson writes, "Either God is served with a single-eyed devotion, or he is not served at all. Attempts at divided loyalty betray, not partial commitment to discipleship, but deep-seated commitment to idolatry."[37]

Either/or. God or Mammon. Earthly treasure versus heavenly treasure. Food and clothing first or God's kingdom first. Fixing our hope on riches or fixing our hope on God.

We can't have it both ways. Choose your Master.

Questions:

1. Why does Jesus have so much to say about money and material things?
2. Does observation of human behavior (people's lifestyles, values, priorities, choices—and the results of those choices) tend to support or negate Jesus' teaching here?
3. To what degree is materialism a problem for Christians today? What evidence do you see for your answer?

4. What is there about money that may tempt us to love it?

5. What are some practical steps we can take to counter the pull of the Mammon Magnet?

6. What Scriptures shed light on whether it is right to earn more money in order to have more to give?

CHAPTER 3

Light vs. Darkness

If we say that we have fellowship with Him and yet walk in the darkness, we lie and do not practice the truth; but if we walk in the Light as He Himself is in the Light, we have fellowship with one another, and the blood of Jesus His Son cleanses us from all sin.

(1 John 1:6-7)

One morning the alarm rang as usual, and I got up and dressed in the dark so as not to disturb Sara. As I started to leave the bedroom, I could see a little light coming from underneath the door. I groped my way toward it and felt for the doorknob. I couldn't find it! I tried the right side of the door and there it was—on the wrong side!

Opening it I was surprised to discover it was the door to our son's room across the hall. Our bedroom door had been open all along, as usual. Normally, we leave a night light on in the bathroom down the hall, but this time it was off, and I was disoriented in the dark.

Spiritual darkness disorients too. "It's all the difference," we say, "between daylight and dark." Hardly anything better illustrates a starker contrast than darkness versus light—a disparity Jesus used in His teaching, as did Peter, Paul, and John. Darkness and light are totally incompatible and mutually exclusive. Paul asks rhetorically, ". . . what fellowship has light with darkness?" (2 Corinthians 6:14). In the spiritual realm, light and darkness have opposite sources, conflicting values, and drastically different outcomes. They are enemies.

Jesus often contrasted two opposites. He spoke of God versus Satan, good versus evil, the wise and foolish builders, the five virgins who were prepared and the five who were not, wheat and tares, the narrow way and the broad, sheep and goats, heaven and hell.

Such sharp dichotomies don't set well with today's postmodern mind. Only two options? Far too confining. Either/or? That's narrow-minded. Good versus evil? How bigoted, intolerant, judgmental.

But that's how Jesus sliced it—take it or leave it.

Walking in the Darkness

Each of us is walking somewhere—either in the light or in the darkness. So what do darkness and light represent? According to Alexander Maclaren, "Light is in all languages the symbol of knowledge, of joy, of purity . . . . Darkness is the type of ignorance, of sorrow, or sin."[38] Donald W. Burdick writes, "Light represents what is good, true and holy, while darkness represents what is evil and false . . . ."[39]

Light is associated with God and goodness, and darkness with Satan and sin (Acts 26:18, 23; Ephesians 6:12; Colossians 1:13). Satan blinds people to the truth, if he can, while God illuminates us through His Son, the Light of the world, and through His gospel (Matthew 4:13-16; John 1:4-9; 8:12; 2 Corinthians 4:4).

Jesus says that some people actually love the darkness (John 3:19). In fact, they prefer it over the light. Darkness is their lifestyle-of-choice. They are not willing to let it go because they love their sins too much. Could anything be more tragic than to be offered light, but to choose darkness?

Leaving the Darkness for the Light

What, specifically, does walking in the darkness include? John says that if we hate our brother, we are walking in darkness (1 John 2:9-10). In addition, Paul says,

> The night is almost gone, and the day is near. Therefore let us lay aside **the deeds of darkness** and put on the armor of light. Let us behave properly as in the day, not in carousing and drunkenness, not in sexual promiscuity and sensuality, not in strife and jealousy (Romans 13:12-13, emphasis added).

... walk no longer just as the Gentiles also walk, in the futility of their mind, being **darkened in their understanding,** excluded from the life of God because of the ignorance that is in them, because of the hardness of their heart . . . (Ephesians 4:17-18).

... **for you were formerly darkness,** but now you are Light in the Lord; walk as children of Light . . . . Do not participate in the **unfruitful deeds of darkness,** but instead even expose them; for it is disgraceful even to speak of the things which are done by them in secret (Ephesians 5:8, 11).

In between these last two passages, Paul mentions specific examples of the "deeds of darkness," which Christians are to lay aside: sensuality, impurity, falsehood, anger, stealing, unwholesome speech, bitterness, slander, malice, greed, etc.

The foundational reference point for our principle is this: ". . . God is Light, and in Him there is no darkness at all" (1 John 1:5). Greek scholars tell us that John uses a double negative here for emphasis: "no darkness at all." God and darkness are totally incompatible. They are exact polar opposites, diametrically opposed and mutually exclusive. God is unadulterated purity, unblemished goodness, incorruptible truth.

That being true, if we walk in the darkness, what then? As Alfred Plummer has observed, "If God is Light, to the exclusion of all darkness, then fellowship with darkness excludes fellowship with Him."[40]

Refuting the Claim

To walk in the light or to walk in the darkness means that either we choose to live in harmony with God's way or Satan's. Since God and Satan are irreconcilable enemies, if we choose God's way, we must decisively reject Satan's. Used as a noun, our *walk* is our behavior, our chosen lifestyle. It's easy to claim to be walking in the Light, but are we really? What if our conduct fails to match our claim? John warns, "If we say that we have fellowship with

Him and yet walk in the darkness, we lie and do not practice the truth . . ." (1 John 1:6). Here John cites two logical conclusions that result if we talk Light, but live dark: 1) we lie, and 2) we do not practice the truth. In other words, do what you say. Practice what you preach. Live it!

Even John the apostle of love could be blunt when he had to be. Nobody likes being called a liar. And yet that's exactly what we are, John says, if we claim fellowship with God but aren't living like it. If that's where we are, John's no-nonsense language is designed to wake us up and shake us out of our self-deception. Some people who live in the darkness have known nothing but darkness and can't imagine what it means to live in the Light. Some know they're in the darkness, but they like it that way, and they make no pretense of being on God's side. Both are tragic situations. But what could be worse than claiming fellowship with God while practicing what God finds intolerable? It's a lie, John says. How many people would be willing to admit, "I love darkness, and I hate the Light"? The cognitive dissonance discussed in the last chapter applies here equally well. There can be no resolution to this inner conflict except genuine repentance.

Also if we claim fellowship with God while walking in the darkness, ". . . we do not practice the truth . . . ." (literally, "we are not doing the truth"). Truth is far more than something to be believed and spoken; it is primarily to be lived, to be done. Un-lived truth cancels out all claims to the contrary:

> By this we know that we have come to know Him, if we keep His commandments. The one who says, "I have come to know Him," and does not keep His commandments, is a liar, and the truth is not in him; but whoever keeps His word, in him the love of God has truly been perfected. By this we know that we are in Him: the one who says he abides in Him ought himself to walk in the same manner as He walked . . . . The one who says he is in the Light and yet hates his brother is in the darkness until now. The one who loves his brother abides in the Light and there is no

cause for stumbling in him. But the one who hates his brother is in the darkness and walks in the darkness, and does not know where he is going because the darkness has blinded his eyes (1 John 2:3-6, 9-11).

In his sermon on 1 John 1:5, Alexander Maclaren said, ". . . the underlying thought is that fellowship with God necessarily involves moral likeness to Him . . . . all high-flying pretensions to communion with God must verify themselves by practical righteousness. That cuts deep into an emotional religion, which . . . produces little purifying effect on the humble details of daily life."[41]

Walking in the Light

In the previous section, we saw a long list of the sins characteristic of walking in the darkness. So what does walking in the Light involve? ". . . for the fruit of the Light consists in all goodness and righteousness and truth . . ." (Ephesians 5:9). More specifically, the new lifestyle includes: telling the truth, controlling one's anger, sharing with those in need, and speaking words that build others up (4:25-29). "Be kind to one another, tender-hearted, forgiving each other, just as God in Christ also has forgiven you" (4:32). People of the Light are "imitators of God, as beloved children" (5:1). They "walk in love" (5:2). They give thanks (5:4).

> . . . that, in reference to your former manner of life, you **lay aside the old self**, which is being corrupted in accordance with the lusts of deceit, and that you **be renewed** in the spirit of your mind, and **put on the new self**, which in the likeness of God has been created in righteousness and holiness of the truth (Ephesians 4:22-24, emphasis added).

I wrote in the margin of this passage of my Bible the three points Joel Shelton emphasized in a series of sermons from Ephesians. They are: Remove, Renew, Replace. Remove the old self. Be renewed in your thinking. Replace the old self with the new.

Unless we undergo that inner renewal, we will not succeed in making a lasting transition from darkness to Light. We must learn to think like people of the Light if we are to live like people of the Light. How does this renewal take place? Paul explains that we must "learn Christ" and be "taught in Him, just as truth is in Jesus" (4:20-21). His teaching retrains our minds to think Light instead of darkness.

Just as claiming fellowship with God while walking in the darkness has two huge drawbacks ("we lie and do not practice the truth"), John cites two tremendous blessings that come to those who walk in the Light (1 John 1:7).

Blessing #1: We have fellowship with one another.

What does "one another" mean? Is it fellowship with God or with fellow Christians? Likely the latter. In every other passage in the New Testament where the Greek word *allēlōn* ("one another") is found, it refers to the horizontal relationships we have with others, a major theme of John's letter. J. W. Roberts explains, ". . . John did not say (as we would expect) that we will then have fellowship with God (unless with one another means between us and God, as seems unlikely). First John 1:3 already pointed out the close relationship between our fellowship with the Father and Son and with one another."[42]

Fellowship with God makes possible fellowship with others in Christ. As Maclaren said, ". . . the only cement that perfectly knits men to each other is their common possession of that light, and the consequent fellowship with God."[43]

Blessing #2: The blood of Jesus His Son cleanses us from all sin.

We receive our initial cleansing by Christ's blood at baptism (Acts 2:38; 22:16). Baptism also puts us into Christ (Romans 6:3-5; Colossians 2:12-13; Galatians 3:27). In this new relationship with Christ, we gain the great advantage of ongoing cleansing for any sins we may commit after baptism. Scholars tell us that the present tense here ("cleanses") conveys a continual action. It has often been compared with the action of wiper blades, which keep the windshield clear as long as needed. In the words of James Burton Coffman,

> This great verse is the source of incredible joy, assurance and consolation to the child of God. He never needs to fear that some impulsive, unintentional, or atypical conduct might overtake him with the result of eternal condemnation. His walking "in the light" can be established by the long term directional thrust of his whole life upon earth and cannot be contradicted and negated by any temporary or insignificant lapse.[44]

The Two Conditions

These two blessings—fellowship and forgiveness—are ours as long as we fulfill two conditions. The first is that "we walk in the Light as He Himself is in the Light." What does this mean? It cannot mean that we never sin. Rather, as Roberts says, "'Walking in the light' implies our sincere effort not to sin."[45] Avoiding sin comes easier when we remember that "He Himself is in the Light" and "in Him there is no darkness at all." He is the Standard for all our values and choices.

When we become His children, we must abandon the darkness for the Light—for good. When Jesus appeared to Saul of Tarsus, He commissioned him to go to the Gentiles:

> . . . to open their eyes so that they may turn from darkness to light and from the dominion of Satan to God, that they may receive forgiveness of sins and an inheritance among those who have been sanctified by faith in Me (Acts 26:18; see Colossians 1:13).

As Peter exhorted those who had left their pagan ways behind to follow Christ, ". . . that you may proclaim the excellencies of Him who has called you out of darkness into His marvelous light . . ." (1 Peter 2:9). Once we realize how dark the darkness is and how marvelous the Light, won't we gladly embrace our new lifestyle?

> . . . for you were formerly darkness, but now you are Light in the Lord; walk as children of Light (for the fruit of the Light consists in all goodness and righteousness and truth), trying to learn what is pleasing to the Lord. Do not participate in the unfruitful deeds of darkness, but instead even expose them; for it is disgraceful even to speak of the things which are done by them in secret. But all things become visible when they are exposed by the light, for everything that becomes visible is light. For this reason it says,
> "Awake, sleeper,
> And arise from the dead,
> And Christ will shine on you."
> (Ephesians 5:8-14; see 1 Thessalonians 5:4-8)

What then is the second condition for receiving the blessings of fellowship and forgiveness? "If we confess our sins, He is faithful and righteous to forgive us our sins and to cleanse us from all unrighteousness" (1 John 1:9). But does this mean confessing to God or to others? It depends. If we have sinned against someone, we need to straighten it out with the one we have wronged—and confess it to God as well. If our sin is known only to God and to us, then we confess it to Him. Simply praying, "Forgive me of my sins," is far too general. Let's be brutally honest, specifically naming our sins, admitting our shame before God: "I lied to my mom when she asked me where I had been." "I committed adultery in my heart when I looked at that pornographic website." "I hurt my wife with my unkind words." "I failed to keep my promise to my friend." "I cheated on my taxes." By coming clean in this way, we refuse to dodge the issue by making excuses or blaming anyone but ourselves. This is part of what it means to humble ourselves.

Sometimes restitution should accompany our repentance, where appropriate (Luke 19:8). But in all cases, when we confess, we acknowledge, admit, and own up to our guilt. We beg for mercy. We seek grace. How reassuring it is to know that if we confess our sins, He promises "to forgive us our sins and to cleanse us from all unrighteousness" (1 John 1:9). All unrighteousness—forgiven. What a comfort!

Sin Prevention

Forgiveness is such a blessing, but we must do all we can to avoid those sins in the future (Psalm 39:1; 119:9,11). Just as it is preferable to prevent a fire than to extinguish one, and to avoid cancer than to find a cure, so it is with sin. Preventing sin is Plan A—this is the ideal for which we should strive. But too often we fall short of the ideal. Thank God for Plan B. As John explains:

PLAN A

"My little children, I am writing these things to you so that you may not sin" (1 John 2:1a).

PLAN B

"And if anyone sins, we have an Advocate with the Father, Jesus Christ the righteous; and He Himself is the propitiation [satisfaction] for our sins; and not for ours only, but also for those of the whole world" (1 John 2:1b-2).

John R. W. Stott offers this corrective:

> It is important to hold these two statements in balance ["that you may not sin" and "if anyone sins"]. It is possible to be both too lenient and too severe towards sin. Too great a lenience would seem almost to encourage sin in the Christian by stressing God's provision for the sinner. An exaggerated severity, on the other hand, would either deny the possibility of a Christian sinning or refuse him forgiveness and restoration if he falls. Both extreme positions are contradicted by John.[46]

As we grow in Christ, let's use Plan A more and more frequently, so that it won't be necessary to resort to Plan B nearly so often.

Fellowship and forgiveness, then, are contingent upon these two ifs:

If we walk in the Light . . . .

If we confess our sins . . . .

Christians are people who have made a decisive break with the darkness so that they can walk in the Light. Having chosen to walk in the Light, how could it possibly be to our advantage to take detours into the darkness? It's dangerous out there. We just might not find our way out. We might not even want to find our way out. May we say with Theodor Haecker, "Everything was so dark in my life, and God illuminated it. Do not forget it, O my heart! Do not forget it!"[47]

The Beauty of Enlightened Lives

Years ago, when my sisters lived in Albuquerque, I enjoyed a custom they have there every Christmas—the luminarias. In fact, in the Lee Acres subdivision where one of my sisters lived, if the residents didn't set out their own luminarias, someone else would. At night, family after family would come driving slowly by, gazing at the beauty.

For all its glowing charm, a luminaria is simply a small paper sack, weighted down with an inch or so of sand in the bottom, and with a small candle set in the sand. They are then placed every two or three feet along sidewalks and curbs, and even on top of the flat-roof adobe-style houses so popular there.

If you've never seen an extensive display of luminarias, you might wonder how a candle in a sack could be all that attractive. But it is! The soft, flickering glow through brown paper, multiplied by hundreds, is a surprisingly impressive sight.

There's a lesson in this. Ordinary people stand out when illuminated by Christ within, especially when banded together with others who also have the glow.

"I am the Light of the world," Jesus said. "You are the light of the world," He told His disciples (John 8:12; Matthew 5:14). A truly Christ-filled life is something to see.

When the apostle Paul arrived in the Roman colony of Philippi, he found a city in spiritual darkness. He then began to preach the good news of Jesus. People responded, and when he left, he left a church.

Later Paul urged them to be "children of God above reproach in the midst of a crooked and perverse generation, *among whom you appear as lights in the world . . .*" (Philippians 2:15, italics added). Christians have been "enlightened" (Hebrews 6:4; 10:32) and are "children of Light" (Ephesians 5:8; see Luke 16:8; John 12:36; 1 Thessalonians 5:5). As Leon Morris says, "Christians do not simply live in the light; they are characterized by light."[48]

The light our current "crooked and perverse generation" needs most is not the enlightenment of education, the illumination of scientific discovery, nor is it the beacon of freedom from political oppression, valuable as all of those are.

The light our world so desperately needs is the light Jesus ignites in the hearts of those who live in Him—the light of salvation, holiness, love, and truth. It is "the Light of life" (John 8:12).

Darkness vs. Light

Reference	Darkness	Light
Proverbs 4:18-19	The way of the wicked is like darkness; they do not know over what they stumble.	The path of the righteous is like the light of dawn, that shines brighter and brighter until the full day.

Reference	Darkness	Light
John 3:19-21	This is the judgment, that the Light has come into the world, and men loved the darkness rather than the Light, for their deeds were evil. For everyone who does evil hates the Light, and does not come to the Light for fear that his deeds will be exposed.	But he who practices the truth comes to the Light, so that his deeds may be manifested as having been wrought in God.
Ephesians 5:8-9	. . . for you were formerly darkness,	but now you are Light in the Lord; walk as children of Light (for the fruit of the Light consists in all goodness and righteousness and truth) . . . .
1 Thessalonians 5:4-5	But you, brethren, are not in darkness, that the day would overtake you like a thief;	for you are all sons of light and sons of day. We are not of night nor of darkness . . . .
1 Peter 2:9	. . . that you may proclaim the excellencies of Him who has called you out of darkness	into His marvelous light . . . .
1 John 1:5-7	. . . God is Light, and in Him there is no darkness at all. If we say that we have fellowship with Him and yet walk in the darkness, we lie and do not practice the truth;	but if we walk in the Light as He Himself is in the Light, we have fellowship with one another, and the blood of Jesus His Son cleanses us from all sin.

Reference	Darkness	Light
1 John 2:9-11	The one who says he is in the Light and yet hates his brother is in the darkness until now . . . . the one who hates his brother is in the darkness and walks in the darkness, and does not know where he is going because the darkness has blinded his eyes.	The one who loves his brother abides in the Light and there is no cause for stumbling in him.

Distinction or Confusion?

As the chart above makes abundantly clear, the contrast between darkness and light should be quite evident to anyone willing to see. Many today, however, are doing all they can to blur the differences. Wouldn't it be greatly to Satan's advantage to promote darkness under the guise of light, thus confusing the differences between them? As Paul warned, ". . . even Satan disguises himself as an angel of light. Therefore it is not surprising if his servants also disguise themselves as servants of righteousness . . ." (2 Corinthians 11:14-15). What Isaiah said so long ago is particularly pertinent to our day:

> Woe to those who call evil good, and good evil;
> *Who substitute darkness for light and light for darkness;*
> Who substitute bitter for sweet and sweet for bitter!
> (Isaiah 5:20, italics added)

Examples of Calling Good Evil, and Evil Good

> Promises of immortal salvation or fear of damnation are both illusory and harmful. They distract humans from present concerns, from self-actualization, and from rectifying social injustices.
>
> –*Humanist Manifesto II* [49]

. . . how shall we respond to the question whether extramarital sex is always wrong? Or even paid sex? Women have done it to feed their families, to pay debts, to serve their countries in counterespionage, to honor a man whom they could not marry. Are we not entitled to say that, depending on the situation, those who break the Seventh Commandment of the old law, even whores, could be doing a good thing—if it is for love's sake, for the neighbor's sake. In short, is there any real "law" of universal weight? The situationist thinks not.

–Joseph Fletcher [50]

Living together before marriage eliminates surprises . . . . People don't buy cars without test driving them first.

....

Once a loathed practice, living together before marriage has become a more common and acceptable trend among couples. Having done it myself, I truly believe living together first has the power to help a couple decide if marriage is right for them, eliminating the potential for divorce and paving the way for a lasting relationships down the line.[51]

Homosexuality is a normal variant of adult sexuality; gay men and lesbians possess the same potential and desire for sustained loving and lasting relationships as heterosexuals, including loving and parenting children. This is supported by hard data, not just opinion.

–Prudence Gourguechon, MD [52]

Porn strokes the ego. Now we get into the core pshcyological [sic] issue at hand. Believe it or not, society today is burdened by a countless number of people who feel lonely, depressed, and downright insufficient. Pornography gives those people the opportunity to release their innermost desires and feel whole again. In short, it strokes their ego. This reduces crime, increases work productivity, and most important of all—it makes people feel better about themselves.[53]

Contrary to anti-choice rhetoric, **abortion does not kill babies or children**. Abortion does not kill persons. Abortion is only performed before a person is formed and long before viability or any consciousness, which is the ultimate determination of personhood.[54]

In a spirit of compassion for all, this manifesto proclaims that every competent adult has the incontestable right to humankind's ultimate civil and personal liberty—the right to die in a manner and at a time of their own choosing. Suicide no longer being a crime, it is unacceptable to prosecute well-meaning people for assisting a suicide.

–Derek Humphry, The Hemlock Society [55]

....

But God's words through Isaiah still stand: "Woe to those who call evil good, and good evil." An anonymous poet's paraphrase of Isaiah's warning gets right to the point:

I dreamed last night that I had come
To dwell in Topsy-Turveydom,
Where vice is virtue, virtue vice,
Where nice is nasty, nasty nice,
Where right is wrong, and wrong is right,
Where white is black, and black is white! [56]

"I dreamed last night . . ." the poet said. Sounds like a nightmare to me!

Questions:

1. Why are light and darkness such fitting symbols of good and evil?

2. Why would a Christian claim fellowship with God while walking in the darkness?

3. Comment on Maclaren's statement, ". . . all high-flying pretensions to communion with God must verify themselves by practical righteousness. That cuts deep into an emotional religion, which . . . produces little purifying effect on the humble details of daily life."

4. What practical steps can we take to prevent ourselves from falling into sin in the first place?

5. Study the Light vs. Darkness chart above and discuss your observations.

6. What are some other examples of substituting light for darkness and darkness for light?

CHAPTER 4

Reaping What We Sow

. . . for whatever a man sows, this he will also reap.

(Galatians 6:7)

W hen my dad was a boy, he learned early the principle of reaping what you sow. Using a magnifying glass one day to focus the sun's rays on a bug or worm, he suddenly felt the back of his neck growing strangely warm. He looked up to see his grandfather standing over him, holding his eyeglasses so as to focus the sun on the young tormentor's neck, giving him a taste of his own medicine.

Life has a way of dishing back what we dish out, whether good or bad. If we treat others right, they are much more likely to respond in kind. If we wrong others, should we be surprised if they wrong us in return? But far more important, God is watching. If we do right by others, God blesses us; if we wrong others, He will hold us accountable. For this dynamic to work, the following would have to be true: 1) God would have to remember all we do, both good and bad, and He does; and 2) someday He must reward or punish accordingly, and He will (2 Corinthians 5:10).

It is truly impressive how often this principle is stressed in Scripture:

He has dug a pit and hollowed it out,
And has fallen into the hole which he made.
His mischief will return upon his own head,
And his violence will descend upon his own pate
(Psalm 7:15-16; see 5:10; 10:2; 57:6; Proverbs 26:27; 28:10).

The nations have sunk down in the pit which they have made;
In the net which they hid, their own foot has been caught.
The LORD has made Himself known;

He has executed judgment.
In the work of his own hands the wicked is snared
(Psalm 9:15-16; see 35:7-8).

. . . he who seeks evil, evil will come to him (Proverbs 11:27b).

Say to the righteous that it will go well with them,
For they will eat the fruit of their actions.
Woe to the wicked! It will go badly with him,
For what he deserves will be done to him (Isaiah 3:10-11).

. . . all those who take up the sword shall perish by the sword
(Matthew 26:52; see Proverbs 1:16-19).

For after all it is only just for God to repay with affliction those
who afflict you . . . (2 Thessalonians 1:6).

For judgment will be merciless to one who has shown no mercy;
mercy triumphs over judgment (James 2:13).

Examples of the Principle

. . . Adoni-bezek fled; and they pursued him and caught him and
cut off his thumbs and big toes. Adoni-bezek said, "Seventy kings
with their thumbs and their big toes cut off used to gather up
scraps under my table; as I have done, so God has repaid me." So
they brought him to Jerusalem and he died there (Judges 1:6-7).

Samuel said [to King Agag of the Amalekites], "As your sword
has made women childless, so shall your mother be childless
among women." And Samuel hewed Agag to pieces before the
LORD at Gilgal (1 Samuel 15:33).

Then Harbonah, one of the eunuchs who were before the king
said, "Behold indeed, the gallows standing at Haman's house fifty
cubits high, which Haman made for Mordecai who spoke good
on behalf of the king!" And the king said, "Hang him on it." So
they hanged Haman on the gallows which he had prepared for
Mordecai . . . (Esther 7:9-10; see 9:25; Daniel 6:6-7, 11-13, 24).

[Addressed to Assyria]
Woe to you, O destroyer,
While you were not destroyed;

And he who is treacherous, while others did not deal treacherously
with him.
As soon as you finish destroying, you will be destroyed;
As soon as you cease to deal treacherously, others will deal
treacherously with you (Isaiah 33:1).

Summon many against Babylon,
All those who bend the bow:
Encamp against her on every side,
Let there be no escape.
Repay her according to her work;
According to all that she has done, so do to her . . .
(Jeremiah 50:29; see 51:56; Psalm 137:8;
Habakkuk 2:8; Revelation 18:6-8).

[Addressed to the nation of Edom]
Because of violence to your brother Jacob,
You will be covered with shame,
And you will be cut off forever.
On the day that you stood aloof,
On the day that strangers carried off his wealth,
And foreigners entered his gate
And cast lots for Jerusalem—
You too were as one of them . . .
As you have done, it will be done to you.
Your dealings will return on your own head (Obadiah 10-11, 15).

What Goes Around . . . .

God has so arranged our world that the wrongs we commit against
one another will sooner or later come ricocheting back. Willem
A. VanGemeren aptly says, "Sin . . . may be likened to a boom-
erang . . . "[57] Keeping this in mind can prevent many a misstep
and spare us countless heartaches down the road.

On the other hand, whatever good we do for others will be
amply rewarded (Matthew 6:3-4; 25:31-46; Mark 9:41; Luke 14:13-
14). God won't forget—He keeps good books (Hebrews 6:10). And

someday the books will be opened (Revelation 20:11-12).

Harvest Time

Few people my age grew up on a farm, but many older people I have known had strong rural roots. I've enjoyed listening to their stories about hoeing the weeds out of the cotton patch and how backbreaking cotton picking can be. Since I grew up in the city, there is so much I don't know about agriculture. I did learn one thing: A farmer explained to me that you plant cotton, but you sow wheat. Nice to know, but I doubt I'll ever do either.

Even urbanites like me who have never driven a plow or operated a combine know that you can't harvest unless you sow, and if you want a wheat crop, you must sow wheat and not something else. According to the first page of the Bible, this is the divine design.

> Then God said, "Let the earth sprout vegetation: plants yielding seed, and fruit trees on the earth bearing fruit *after their kind* with seed in them"; and it was so. The earth brought forth vegetation, plants yielding seed *after their kind*, and trees bearing fruit with seed in them, *after their kind*; and God saw that it was good" (Genesis 1:11-12, italics added).

Like produces like. What works in agriculture also works in everyday life. You reap what you sow. This principle is just as certain and inevitable as the literal seedtime/harvest law God set in motion in the beginning and then reinforced following the Flood (Genesis 8:22).

And yet many live as though they don't believe they will reap what they sow. To counter such thinking Paul issues this warning, **"Do not be deceived**, God is not mocked; for whatever a man sows, <u>this</u> he will also reap" (Galatians 6:7, emphasis added).

The sow/reap principle is based on the concept that the choices we make have inevitable and corresponding outcomes, for good or bad. Satan does not want us to believe this. He will deny or downplay the consequences, and instead he promises good fruit from sowing to the flesh (Genesis 3:1-5). So whom will we believe: God or Satan?

"The danger of deception is very real. For one thing the interval between the sowing and the reaping is much longer than in the natural world, and the connection between them is not clearly seen."[58]

"Do not be deceived," Paul warns. One day Sara received a phone call saying that the warranty on our car was about to expire. When the caller asked for the make and model of our car, Sara said, "If you don't know that, this must not be a legitimate call." The caller hung up. *Caveat emptor* (Let the buyer beware). If we must be alert to scams, how much more do we need to watch out for the one "who deceives the whole world" (Revelation 12:9). Jesus labels him "a liar and the father of lies" (John 8:44). Satan wants us to believe we can sow to the flesh yet not reap corruption. Many fall into this trap because they are only too glad to believe it.

When We Sow to the Flesh

What does *flesh* mean in this context? The word is used in several senses in the New Testament—both literal and metaphorical, as Morris explains:

> "The flesh" may stand for the whole of this physical existence . . . . There is no blame attached to this, and, indeed, Christ is said more than once to have been "in the flesh" (Ephesians 2:15; 1 Peter 3:18; 1 John 4:2, etc.) . . . . The life that Paul the Christian now lived was "in the flesh" (Galatians 2:20).
>
> But, by definition, the flesh is the earthly part of man. It has its "lusts" and its "desires" (Ephesians 2:3) . . . . The flesh in this sense denotes the whole personality of man as organized in the wrong direction, as directed to earthly pursuits rather than the service of God.[59]

A Harvest Nobody Wants

Paul warns that if we sow to the flesh we will reap corruption

(Galatians 6:8). Literally, corruption refers to that which is perishable and subject to decay (1 Corinthians 15:42). Once when I tried to look up something in one of my computer files, a message popped up on the screen: "Word was unable to read this document. It may be corrupt." Corruption—whether in a computer, a corpse, or our own conscience—is a dismal situation indeed.

As used in our text, corruption refers to moral degradation or destruction, the bitter fruit of sin. God means for us to "become partakers of the divine nature, having escaped the corruption that is in the world by lust" (2 Peter 1:4). Peter warns of the false teachers who

> entice by fleshly desires, by sensuality, those who barely escape from the ones who live in error, promising them freedom while they themselves are *slaves of corruption*; for by what a man is overcome, by this he is enslaved (2 Peter 2:18-19, italics added).

The sow/reap principle is found in the Old Testament as well: "He who sows iniquity will reap vanity . . ." (Proverbs 22:8). "For they sow the wind and they reap the whirlwind" (Hosea 8:7). And then, positively, "Sow with a view to righteousness, reap in accordance with kindness . . ." (Hosea 10:12; see Proverbs 11:18).

What we sow today we will reap someday. How many who sow to the flesh fully expect to reap corruption?

Considering the Consequences

Hindsight, we say, is a better teacher than foresight. But what if we could know in advance exactly what we will reap? Would Adam and Eve have partaken of the tree of the knowledge of good and evil if they could have foreseen the awful consequences of their choice for themselves and all their descendants (Romans 5:12)? Would Reuben have committed fornication if he knew he would lose all the privileges that would have been his by right as the firstborn son (Genesis 49:3-4; 1 Chronicles 5:1)? Would the ten spies have brought their discouraging report if they had seen in advance that it would result in their deaths and in the exclusion of thousands of their fellow Israelites from the great blessings God had in store for the faithful (Numbers 13-14)? Would David have taken Bathsheba if he could have foreseen what evils would come crashing down on his head as a direct consequence of his lust (2 Samuel 11:1-27; 12:1-23; 13:1-39; 18:32-33; Psalm 51)? Would the Rich Young Ruler have turned his back on Jesus if he had understood at the time what he was truly forfeiting (Mark 10:17-31)? More to the point, would we make the sinful choices we do if we could look ahead and see where Temptation Trail is taking us? In choosing to sin, don't we prove to be our own worst enemies?

Many years ago my dad and I traveled to Dallas, and on one building along the way was this sign:

An evidence of immaturity is the tendency to do what feels good *now* without regard to the possible consequences. How many of us wish we had planned ahead?

As Moses was preparing Israel for entering Canaan he taught them a song. The lyrics include these lines: "For they are a nation void of counsel, neither is there any understanding in them. O that they were wise, *that they understood this, that they would consider their latter end!*(Deuteronomy 32:28-29 KJV, italics added; see Proverbs 5:7-11)

Centuries later, after the city of Jerusalem had fallen to the Babylonians as a consequence of rejecting God, Jeremiah lamented, "She [Jerusalem] did not consider her future" (Lamentations 1:9). The note in the margin of the New American Standard Bible says that the literal translation of this is that Jerusalem "did not remember her latter end." Jerusalem's end was a sad one, all the more tragic because it was so avoidable. They had been amply warned about what would happen if they did not repent, but they chose to ignore the warnings.

We can learn from them if we will. God's Word provides us with a clear picture of how it will be for us if we choose God's way—and how it will be for us if we choose our own. We reap what we sow. There is no question that each of us has a "latter end." The only question is: Will we consider our latter end so that it will be a happy one, as God intended? G. B. Shelburne III observes:

> "If only . . . ." Are there any sadder words? If only I had spent time with the children while they were young, refused that last promotion, respected my parents' love, avoided that first drink, ignored that flirtation, given my life to Christ. Today's numbing losses grow from yesterday's tragic choices.
>
> I have a friend who was poised to sacrifice his family for an affair. I said to him, "This path will end in tears and regret. I know people who would give anything if they could still be where you are, not yet having made the jump. Still able to turn back."
>
> We have all made choices we now regret. God does not stop loving us. He accepts our repentance, holds us and gives worth to our lives. But how much better to have taken the forks which lead to good and avoid heartbreak. [60]

Sad Harvesters

Paul Laurence Dunbar has written,

> This is the debt I pay
> Just for one riotous day,
> Years of regret and grief,
> Sorrow without relief. [61]

The Bible is filled with examples of those who could no doubt echo Dunbar's lament:

> Esau sowed to his appetite and reaped the loss of his birthright (Genesis 25:27-34; Hebrews 12:16).

Joseph's brothers sowed to envy, and years later they were still reaping the accusations of their guilty consciences (Genesis 37; 42:21-22; 50:15-18; Acts 7:9).

Peter sowed to his cowardice and reaped bitter tears of regret (Luke 22:31-34, 54-62).

"Do not be deceived, God is not mocked . . . ." He means what He says—whether we believe it or not. Why the warning about being deceived? If we don't want to believe that we reap what we sow, we will likely be deceived into thinking that we will not reap corruption.

So what is involved in sowing to the flesh? Paul gets quite specific:

Now the deeds of the flesh are evident, which are: immorality, impurity, sensuality, idolatry, sorcery, enmities, strife, jealousy, outbursts of anger, disputes, dissensions, factions, envying, drunkenness, carousing, and things like these, of which I forewarn you, just as I have forewarned you, that those who practice such things will not inherit the kingdom of God (Galatians 5:19-21).

Cecil May III writes:

The sin list has not changed. Sin lists are recorded in Romans 1:26-31; 1 Corinthians 5:11 and 6:9-10; Galatians 5:19-21; Ephesians 4:25-5:5; Colossians 3:3-5; and Revelation 21:8. The actions and attitudes that made the sin lists 2000 years ago are still sin. Culturally, we have moved some of those items off the culturally disapproved list, but God has not moved them off his sin list. In particular, the world around us has of late changed its views regarding the sinfulness of many sexual transgressions. Still, all the sin lists above include sexual immorality, and five of the seven start off their lists with sexual immorality or some specified form of sexual sin.[62]

Is There a Way Out?

If we find some of our own sins in these lists, what then can we do about it? A few verses later Paul says, "Now those who belong to

Christ Jesus have crucified the flesh with its passions and desires" (Galatians 5:24; see 2:20; 6:14). This crucifixion of the flesh is that daily determination to put our old ways behind us and live instead by the Spirit. Is this too hard? At least two factors can put this in perspective. First, it is encouraging to realize that this option is available. Instead of being doomed forever to being dominated by the flesh, we have a way out! The good news is: "Therefore if anyone is in Christ, he is a new creature; the old things passed away; behold, new things have come" (2 Corinthians 5:17).

Second, we don't have to make this dramatic change on our own. God supplies us with all the resources and help we need to put our old self to death and become the new creature God meant for us to be. He equips us with spiritual armor to defeat Satan (Ephesians 6:10-17). He grants us the indwelling Holy Spirit to strengthen us (Ephesians 3:16). He furnishes us with His Word to instruct and correct us (2 Timothy 3:14-17). His gives us prayer "so that we may receive mercy and find grace to help in time of need" (Hebrews 4:16). He provides us with brothers and sisters in Christ as our family to teach and encourage us, "so that none of you will be hardened by the deceitfulness of sin" (Hebrews 3:12-13; see 10:24-25). We are not alone. We're all in this together!

The change we experience doesn't happen overnight. It is a lifelong process of learning and growing. And if we keep working God's program, it gets better and better. "But we all, with unveiled face, beholding as in a mirror the glory of the Lord, are being transformed into the same image from glory to glory, just as from the Lord, the Spirit" (2 Corinthians 3:18).

When We Sow to the Spirit

Having examined the warning, "For the one who sows to his own flesh will from the flesh reap corruption," let us now see how the second half of the principle can work to our great advantage: ". . . but the one who sows to the Spirit will from the Spirit reap

RIGHTSIDE-UP LIVING IN AN UPSIDE-DOWN WORLD

eternal life" (Galatians 6:8). In both the warning part of the principle and the promise part, reaping follows sowing, and what is reaped is the direct result of what is sown: ". . . for whatever a man sows, this he will also reap."

So how do we sow to the Spirit? We do it by living in harmony with what the Spirit desires and has revealed in the Scriptures (which He inspired). We mold our thoughts, words, and actions to conform to the values of the Spirit. By doing this we harvest a first-class crop: "But the fruit of the Spirit is love, joy, peace, patience, kindness, goodness, faithfulness, gentleness, self-control; against such things there is no law" (Galatians 5:22-23). What a contrast to the deeds of the flesh listed in the previous three verses! Flesh and Spirit are as opposite as they can be (Romans 8:6-8, 12-13; Galatians 5:16-17). As James Allen has written,

Good thoughts bear good fruit, bad thoughts bear bad fruit.[63]

. . . nothing can come from corn but corn, nothing from nettles but nettles. Men understand this law in the natural world, and work with it; but few understand it in the mental and moral world (though its operation there is just as simple and undeviating), and they, therefore, do not co-operate with it.[64]

So how does your garden grow?

It is easy to sow to the flesh; it can be quite the challenge to sow to the Spirit and keep doing it consistently—but oh, how worth the price! Stephen R. Covey asks, "Did you ever consider how ridiculous it would be to try to cram on a farm—to forget to plant in the spring, play all summer and then cram in the fall to bring in the harvest? The farm is a natural system. The price must be paid and the process followed. You always reap what you sow; there is no short cut."[65]

In the verse immediately following our text on sowing to the Spirit, Paul cautions against slacking off on the sowing:

Let us not lose heart in doing good, for in due time we will reap if we do not grow weary. So then, while we have opportunity, let us do good to all people, and especially to those who are of the household of the faith (Galatians 6:9-10).

In other passages in Galatians Paul refers to various ways of doing good, including helping the poor (2:10), serving fellow Christians (5:13), restoring an erring brother (6:1), bearing one another's burdens (6:2), and sharing with those who teach the word (6:6). Some but not all of these involve financial help. Yet all are ways of sowing to the Spirit. Corresponding to each is the promised harvest. God sees and remembers when we meet needs, financial or otherwise, and He will reward. ". . . for whatever a man sows, this he will also reap."

Flesh vs. Spirit

Passage	Sowing to the Flesh	Sowing to the Spirit
Romans 8:5	For those who are according to the flesh set their minds on the things of the flesh . . .	. . . but those who are according to the Spirit, the things of the Spirit.
Romans 8:6	For the mind set on the flesh is death . . .	. . . but the mind set on the Spirit is life and peace . . .
Romans 8:7-10	. . . because the mind set on the flesh is hostile toward God; for it does not subject itself to the law of God, for it is not even able to do so, and those who are in the flesh cannot please God.	However, you are not in the flesh but in the Spirit, if indeed the Spirit of God dwells in you . . . . If Christ is in you, though the body is dead because of sin, yet the spirit is alive because of righteousness.
Romans 8:13	. . . for if you are living according to the flesh, you must die . . .	. . . but if by the Spirit you are putting to death the deeds of the body, you will live.

Passage	Sowing to the Flesh	Sowing to the Spirit
Galatians 5:19-23	Now the deeds of the flesh are evident, which are: immorality, impurity, sensuality, idolatry, sorcery, enmities, strife, jealousy, outbursts of anger, disputes, dissensions, factions, envying, drunkenness, carousing and things like these, of which I forewarn you, just as I have forewarned you, that those who practice such things will not inherit the kingdom of God.	But the fruit of the Spirit is love, joy, peace, patience, kindness, goodness, faithfulness, gentleness, self-control; against such things there is no law.
Galatians 6:7-10	Do not be deceived, God is not mocked; for whatever a man sows, this he will also reap. For the one who sows to his own flesh will from the flesh reap corruption . . .	. . . but the one who sows to the Spirit will from the Spirit reap eternal life. Let us not lose heart in doing good, for in due time we will reap if we do not grow weary. So then, while we have opportunity, let us do good to all people, and especially to those who are of the household of the faith.

Conclusion

Each of us is a sower. Each of us is a reaper. We each decide what kind of sower we will be. And that decision determines what kind of reaper we will be. If we choose to sow to the flesh, are we prepared for the inevitable harvest? As Covey says, "While we are free to choose our actions, we are not free to choose the consequences of those actions. Consequences are governed by natural law . . . . We can decide to step in front of a fast-moving train, but we cannot decide what will happen when the train hits us."[66]

Apparently some think they can sow to the flesh and still reap eternal life. Jesus warns that many travel the broad way to destruction, but only a few take the narrow road that leads to life (Matthew 7:13-14). How strongly do we believe that "the one who sows to the Spirit will from the Spirit reap eternal life"? Do we "lose heart in doing good" because we don't fully trust God's promise that "in due time we will reap if we do not grow weary"? Growing weary is a faith problem. The Christian who grows weary of doing good to the point of giving up is essentially saying, "God, I do not believe you!" But if we keep doing good, someday God's promise will no longer be a promise—it will be joyous reality.

A farmer who had just gone through a prolonged drought told me that he did get in one good wheat harvest, and his crop insurance helped with the rest. Although crop insurance cannot guarantee a good crop, it does cover loss. God's promise is better than that. It is not insurance but assurance, a 100 percent fail-proof warranty that if we work God's program, we will reap eternal life. God's integrity stands behind His promise, and He has a flawless track record in the promise-keeping department. Abraham shows us how to respond to God's guarantees: ". . . with respect to the promise of God, he did not waver in unbelief but grew strong in faith, giving glory to God, and being fully assured that what God had promised, He was able also to perform" (Romans 4:20-21).

. . . for whatever a man sows, this he will also reap. You can count on it.

Questions:

1. What qualities of God are demonstrated by the principle that we reap what we sow?

2. Why does sowing to the flesh come so easily to most people?

3. How does the "long view" help us decide what kind of sower we will be?

4. Is it possible for a Christian to forfeit eternal life?
   (1 Timothy 5:5-6; 2 Peter 2:20-22)

5. What can we do to keep faithful? (Romans 8:12-13;
   1 Corinthians 15:58; Revelation 2:11)

6. If we do fall away, what must we do? (James 5:19-20;
   Revelation 3:1-3)

CHAPTER 5

Sowing Little, Sowing Much

. . . he who sows sparingly will also reap sparingly,
and he who sows bountifully will also reap bountifully.

(2 Corinthians 9:6)

S ara loves to grow things, and for several years we had a garden plot about 30'× 30' in our backyard. But as the trees continued to grow to the point that the plants weren't getting enough sun, she was then limited mostly to a small strip along the back fence. Because she couldn't plant as much, we didn't harvest as much. Recently, however, as a result of having a large tree removed, sunshine has replaced the shade. So now we can plant more—and harvest more.

The New Testament uses the metaphor of sowing and reaping in several different senses. As we saw in the last chapter, if we sow to the flesh, we will reap corruption, but if we sow to the Spirit, we will reap eternal life. Also, the seed of the gospel is sown in people's hearts (Luke 8:5, 11), and when they respond in faith, this is the harvest (Matthew 9:37-38; John 4:36-38). But in 2 Corinthians 9:6 Paul uses *sow* to mean give, and *reap* to refer to the blessings that come back to the giver.

> The one who is taught the word is to **share all good things** with the one who teaches him . . . . for whatever a man sows, this he will also reap. For the one who sows to his own flesh will from the flesh reap corruption, but the one who sows to the Spirit will from the Spirit reap eternal life. **Let us not lose heart in doing good, for in due time we will reap if we do not grow weary. So then, while we have opportunity, let us do good** to all people, and especially to those who are of the household of the faith (Galatians 6:6-10, emphasis added).

Doing good to others by sharing our resources with them

is one way we sow to the Spirit. Paul cautions against growing weary of serving others. How easy it is to fall prey to what has been called "compassion fatigue," but if we persevere in doing good, Paul says, the harvest (reward) of our sharing will make it all worthwhile. Remembering this can help prevent the burnout that so often accompanies benevolence.

Regarding our text, ". . . he who sows sparingly will also reap sparingly, and he who sows bountifully will also reap bountifully," Philip Hughes comments, "The important lesson . . . is that to give is to sow. What is given is not lost, but, like the seed sown by the farmer, contrary to all appearances it possesses the potency of life and increase . . . . The sphere of giving, then, presents no exception to the inexorable rule, valid in the moral no less than in the agricultural realm, that a man reaps according to the manner of his sowing . . . ."[67]

In farming and gardening, due to conditions beyond our control, it is possible to sow a lot but reap little or nothing. But God assures us that when we give generously, we will reap much. That's the promise. His pledge is backed by His absolute power and integrity, and it is amply confirmed by countless people who have tried out God's promise and found it wonderfully true.

Why Sparingly?

Why do many Christians give far less than they could? Let's consider three common hindrances to generosity. As we do, let's examine ourselves to see if any of these hindrances could apply to us.

Hindrance #1: Lack of Faith

Some are afraid that if they give generously they can't pay the bills or have enough for a "rainy day." Could they be listening more to the stock market report than to God's promises, or could they be paying more attention to their dwindling bank balance than to God's inexhaustible resources? Is their problem a shortage of funds—or a shortage of faith? Will I hurt myself by generous giving? Unbelief says *yes*. Faith says *no*. Will God take care of me if I sow bountifully? Unbelief says *no*. Faith says *yes*.

Are we focused more on God's promises or on outward circumstances? "He who watches the wind will not sow and he who looks at the clouds will not reap" (Ecclesiastes 11:4). Though a farmer must listen to the weather report, it is possible to wait too long to plant. Even when conditions are not ideal, without sowing there is no reaping. If General Dwight D. Eisenhower had waited for perfect weather, D-Day might never have turned out as it did.

> There is a tide in the affairs of men,
> Which, taken at the flood, leads on to fortune;
> Omitted, all the voyage of their life
> Is bound in shallows and in miseries.[68]

There is something about keeping that impoverishes; there is something about giving that enriches. The rich young ruler kept his wealth and was sad (Matthew 19:16-22). The Macedonians gave out of poverty and were glad (2 Corinthians 8:2). Strange, isn't it? Or is it? This is the way God designed it. He wants us to know the joy!

Hindrance #2: Lack of Love

After citing the exceptional benevolence of their brethren in the neighboring province of Macedonia, Paul urges the Corinthians to follow their example:

> I am not speaking this as a command, but as **proving** through the earnestness of others **the sincerity of your love** also (2 Corinthians 8:8, emphasis added).

> Therefore openly before the churches, show them **the proof of your love** and of our reason for boasting about you (2 Corinthians 8:24).

> For the ministry of this service is not only fully supplying the needs of the saints, but is also overflowing through many thanksgivings to God. Because of **the proof given by this ministry,** they will glorify God for your obedience to your confession of the gospel of Christ and for the liberality of your contribution to them and to all . . . (2 Corinthians 9:12-13).

Prove your love! The Corinthians could prove their love by generosity. Love and giving go well together: both aim for the good of others. Giving is love in action. When we truly love, giving comes naturally. A man braves a potential explosion to save a stranger from a burning car. A woman donates a kidney to save her brother's life. A child, moved by a missionary's report on the dire conditions of street children in Cambodia, takes up a collection from church members. Such noble expressions of selflessness are reflections of the Ultimate Sacrifice: "For God so loved the world, that He gave His only begotten Son . . . ." John 3:16 speaks of God's love-gift, but the less familiar 1 John 3:16 speaks of Christ's love-gift:

> We know love by this, that He laid down His life for us; and we ought to lay down our lives for the brethren. But whoever has the world's goods, and sees his brother in need and closes his heart against him, how does the love of God abide in Him? Little children, let us not love with word or with tongue, but in deed and truth.

In other words, as Paul said, ". . . show them the proof of your love." Expressing mere verbal well-wishes to someone in need leaves them just as needy as before (James 2:15-16). On the other hand, giving, when unaccompanied by love, is meaningless (1 Corinthians 13:3). But love that demonstrates genuine sacrifice reflects the self-surrendering love of Christ (2 Corinthians 8:1-5, 8).

Hindrance #3: Love of Money

Garry Friesen may well be right in asserting, "The greatest

threat to generous giving is not poverty, but covetousness (2 Corinthians 9:5; Luke 12:13-34; Acts 5:1-10)." [69] According to T. Pierce Brown, covetousness (greed) "is one of the most dangerous and insidious sins known to man. Men have confessed to murder, lying, adultery, and almost every sin known. Have you ever heard one confess to covetousness?" [70]

Money is a dangerous thing, but it also has tremendous potential for good. Paul contrasts the bad and good ways of looking at money:

> But those who want to get rich fall into temptation and a snare and many foolish and harmful desires which plunge men into ruin and destruction. For the love of money is a root of all sorts of evil, and some by longing for it have wandered away from the faith and pierced themselves with many griefs . . . . Instruct those who are rich in this present world not to be conceited or to fix their hope on the uncertainty of riches, but on God, who richly supplies us with all things to enjoy. Instruct them to do good, to be rich in good works, to be generous and ready to share, storing up for themselves the treasure of a good foundation for the future, so that they may take hold of that which is life indeed (1 Timothy 6:9-10, 17-19).

Those Who Love Money

Those who want to get rich ➡	fall into temptation
	fall into a snare
	fall into many foolish and harmful desires ➡ ruin and destruction
The love of money ➡	is a root of all sorts of evil
Some by longing for money ➡	have wandered away from the faith
	have pierced themselves with many griefs

Those Who Fix Their Hope on God

Those who are rich in this present world ➡ should not be conceited or fix their hope on the uncertainty of riches but *should* fix their hope on God

Instruct
them: to do good

to be rich in good works

to be generous and
ready to share ➡ storing up for themselves the treasure

of a good foundation for the future

so that they may take hold of that which is life indeed

The ultimate outcomes of these opposite value systems are "ruin and destruction" on one hand, and "the treasure of a good foundation for the future" on the other. How do we avoid ruin? How do we obtain our treasure? By sharing. "We cannot serve God and mammon; but we can serve God with mammon." [71]

In Paul's words to Timothy above, his instruction "to do good, to be rich in good works, to be generous and ready to share" is equivalent to bountiful sowing, and the promise of "storing up for themselves the treasure of a good foundation for the future" is bountiful reaping.

Hindrance or Hurdle?

Having looked at three common hindrances to generous giving (lack of faith, lack of love, and love of money), can we honestly say that we have not been affected by any of them? Though it is one thing to identify these common hindrances, it is quite another to admit that we are hindered by any of them. But if, after honest soul-searching, we recognize that the shoe fits, what can we do about it?

First, the good news: We are not stuck with any spiritual deficiency, no matter what it is. The Christian life is one of overcoming the world, not being overcome by it. We can repent. We can change and grow. God provides us with all the resources we need to strengthen our faith in His promises and develop a generous spirit (2 Peter 1:3).

Second, although Satan can put hindrances in our path to make us stumble, let's view them as hurdles to be cleared. A hurdle is for jumping over, not for tripping over. Those who successfully negotiate the hurdles are all the stronger for it. We can learn to sow bountifully, even if we aren't there yet.

Why Bountifully?

What can we learn from the sowing/reaping analogy? Commenting on our principle in 2 Corinthians 9:6, Philip E. Hughes observes, "Outwardly the seed may be small and insignificant, but inwardly its potential is immense. The seed which God supplies must be scattered, it must be sown beneath the ground, that is, it must become to all appearances lost, before its potential can be realized and the manifold blessing of a harvest enjoyed." [72]

What role does faith play in our giving? In giving all she owned, the poor widow whom Jesus observed definitely qualified as a liberal giver because her gift, though monetarily small, was proportionally huge when compared with all those who deposited large sums that same day in the temple treasury (Luke 21:1-4). What kind of faith must she have had to trust God that much? Since Jesus knew she gave her all, and since He spoke for His Father, would God have let her go hungry?

In the Sermon on the Mount, Jesus taught that those who worry about having enough to eat or wear are people "of little faith" (Matthew 6:30). Can't we trust our Father to provide? "But seek first His kingdom and His righteousness, and all these things [your daily necessities] will be added to you" (Matthew

6:33). By giving generously we are saying, "Father, I trust You to keep Your promise to provide for me."

As far as I know, the United States is the only nation that has "In God We Trust" inscribed on its currency. Four simple, one-syllable words, but how profound! It's both fitting and ironic that this motto appears on the very commodity in which too many place their trust. If we really do trust in God, however, we need not worry about our Father's provision when we give generously. Consider this faith-challenge from Mac Layton: "Many think of their giving to the Lord as true sacrifice. They think they will never see their money again. This is false giving, giving without returns, and without faith in the Lord of the harvest. The Lord calls on us to know that our giving to Him is a valuable investment with both earthly and heavenly returns, the wisest exchange in the market of life!"[73]

"God Is Able"

But great givers don't give just so God will bless them. They give because they know they can afford to. They can afford to because God is their financier, and that means they will never run short. If we lived in a closed system, we would be limited to whatever resources we had. But when we factor God into it, we can then relax in the assurance that He will intervene in our world and enable us to have whatever we need. He sometimes provides in strange and mysterious ways. We may not know how He does it, nor do we need to understand it. All we have to do is trust Him to work it out His way and in His own good time. According to Paul, God is "able to do far more abundantly beyond all that we ask or think, according to the power that works within us . . ." (Ephesians 3:20).

Believe it!

Many Happy Returns

The Scriptures, both Old and New Testaments, assure us that when we give to God, He will more than make it up to us. He is the Great Compensator. Desperate for a child, Hannah promised God that if He would grant her request for a son, she would give him back to God. After God gave her the son she prayed for, she kept her promise, devoting her young son Samuel to God's service. God then compensated her with five more children (1 Samuel 2:20-21). When a poor Gentile widow gave Elijah the last bit of food she and her son had to eat, God provided for the three of them for the duration of the famine (1 Kings 17:8-16). When a lad gave Jesus his lunch, Jesus multiplied those five loaves and two fish into enough to satisfy thousands of hungry people, with enough left over to fill twelve baskets (John 6:5-13). Guess who got to eat his fill?

Jesus challenged the Rich Young Ruler to sell his possessions, give to the poor, and become His disciple, promising him treasure in heaven. Unwilling to put Jesus' promise to the test, the young man walked sadly away. In making this choice, he would never know how it would have turned out for him if only he had taken Christ up on His offer.

After he had gone, Peter asked Jesus, "Behold, we have left everything and followed You; what then will there be for us?" (Matthew 19:27). Jesus answered:

> Truly I say to you, there is no one who has left house or brothers or sisters or mother or father or children or farms, for My sake and for the gospel's sake, but that he will receive a hundred times as much now in the present age, houses and brothers and sisters and mothers and children and farms, along with persecutions; and in the age to come, eternal life (Mark 10:28-30).

Wendell Winkler said it well: "Let us remember that our Father is not trying to make us poor; rather, he is trying to make us rich!"[74] Talk about compensation! Can we ever lose, obeying God?

Our principle, ". . . he who sows bountifully will also reap bountifully," is from Paul's two-chapter treatise on the great collection he was raising among Gentile churches for the poor Jewish brethren in Jerusalem. Colin Kruse comments, "The sowing and reaping . . . refer to the contribution the Corinthians are to make and the results of that contribution respectively. The bountiful 'reaping' Paul hopes to see as a result of their bountiful 'sowing' is described in vv. 9-14." [75]

Note what they could expect to harvest:

> . . . as it is written, "He scattered abroad, He gave to the poor, His righteousness endures forever." **Now He who supplies seed to the sower and bread for food will supply and multiply your seed for sowing and increase the harvest of your righteousness; you will be enriched in everything for all liberality, which through us is producing thanksgiving to God.** For the ministry of this service is not only fully supplying the needs of the saints, but is also **overflowing through many thanksgivings to God. Because of the proof given by this ministry, they will glorify God** for your obedience to your confession of the gospel of Christ and for the liberality of your contribution to them and to all, **while they also, by prayer on your behalf, yearn for you** because of the surpassing grace of God in you (2 Corinthians 9:9-14, emphasis added).

These verses indicate that the reaping is in three dimensions: 1) God is glorified, 2) the recipients are blessed, and 3) the givers are richly rewarded. What more could one ask?

Is It Wrong to Motivate Givers with the Hope of Reward?

According to William Barclay, "The New Testament is an extremely practical book and one of its great features is that it is never afraid of the reward motive." [76] As evidence, consider just four of many promises that pertain to giving:

> There is one who scatters, and yet increases all the more,
> And there is one who withholds what is justly due, and yet it results only in want.

The generous man will be prosperous,
And he who waters will himself be watered (Proverbs 11:24-25).

One who is gracious to a poor man lends to the LORD,
And He will repay him for his good deed (Proverbs 19:17).

He who is generous will be blessed,
For he gives some of his food to the poor (Proverbs 22:9).

Give, and it will be given to you. They will pour into your lap a
good measure—pressed down, shaken together, and running
over. *For by your standard of measure it will be measured to you
in return* (Luke 6:38, italics added).

Our principle, ". . . he who sows bountifully will also reap bountifully," is additional evidence. It guarantees tremendous blessings to the generous giver.

Nineteenth-century Princeton scholar Charles Hodge has written:

. . . human wisdom says it is wrong to appeal to any selfish motive.
The wisdom of God, while teaching the entire abnegation of self,
and requiring a man even to hate his own life when in conflict
with the glory of God, tells all who thus deny themselves that
they thereby most effectually promote their own interests . . . .
it is right to present to men the divinely ordained consequences
of their actions as motives to control their conduct. It is right
to tell men that obedience to God, devotion to his glory and
the good of others, will effectually promote their own welfare.[77]

God promised the widow that if she would feed Elijah first, even though she had only enough left for one more meal, she and her son would never go hungry. She believed God and acted accordingly. In contrast, Jesus promised the Rich Young Ruler that if he would sell his possessions and give to the poor, he would have treasure in heaven, but he just couldn't bring himself to do it. He heard Jesus say, "sell" and "give," but evidently the promise "you will have treasure in heaven" didn't register. He heard cost, but did he hear compensation? Apparently he had eyes to see his earthly wealth, but lacked eyes of faith to see the far greater treasure he could have had. And so by turning his back on Jesus, he forfeited a far greater treasure than what he kept. What he did keep he would eventually lose—all of it—when he died, if not sooner. As Charles Caleb Colton put it, "He that will not permit his wealth to do any good to others while he is alive, prevents it from doing any good to himself when he is dead; and . . . cuts himself off from the truest pleasure here, and the highest happiness hereafter." [78]

> Oh what is earth, that we should build
> Our houses here, and seek concealed
> Poor treasure, and add field to field,
> And heap to heap and store to store,
> Still grasping more and seeking more,
> While step by step Death moves near the door?
> —Christina G. Rossetti [79]

The Choice We Make

Take a good hard look at your giving: judging from the amount you sow, what can you expect to reap?

What kind of harvest will we reap if we sow bountifully?

1. We will enjoy God's favor (2 Corinthians 9:6-7; Philippians 4:18; Hebrews 13:16).

2. We will know the joy that only the generous experience (2 Corinthians 8:1-5).

3. We will have all of our daily needs met—guaranteed (Matthew 6:33).

4. God will more than compensate any loss suffered for His sake (Mark 10:28-30).

5. We will have treasure in heaven (Matthew 6:19-21).

Do we doubt it? Doubters sow sparingly, if at all; true believers sow bountifully. What kind of harvest can each expect? Wouldn't it be true to say that those who have not yet learned to give generously, proportionately, and consistently are depriving themselves of some mighty rich blessings? If you doubt it, please take the time to look up the passages cited a few lines above, and then ask yourself, "Would God lie to me?"

Here's an assignment: Find three liberal givers and ask them if they regret having given so much, and listen to what they say. Have they always given generously? If not, what convinced them to start? What advice would they have for someone who is hesitant to give as the Bible teaches?

There are at least three ways we can learn to become bountiful sowers: 1) from what God promises in His word, 2) from our observation of how bountiful givers have prospered, and, best of all, 3) from our own experience. Once we take God at His word and give His promises a fair test, we, too, will know that bountiful sowing does indeed result in bountiful reaping, just as God has promised.

At age 86, looking back on how God had richly blessed him financially and given him many opportunities to share with others, A. M. Burton testified from his own long experience with God:

> It seems to me that my rewards for giving have been greatly increased by giving as I have been prospered and at the time I have been prospered—not waiting to will my goods to noble causes and deserving persons to enjoy after my death. Now, while I yet live, I have been privileged to see the results of my giving, and I can testify that it is one of the greatest joys the heart can know.[80]

Questions:

1. Review the three common hindrances to generosity discussed above. Can you think of other hindrances besides these?

2. What can help us develop greater faith in God's promises?

3. Read 2 Corinthians 8-9, and list all the ways Paul uses to motivate the Corinthians to be generous.

4. What might be included in the "all sorts of evil" that love of money can lead to?

5. What percentage of your income are you currently giving to God?

6. What expenditures could you eliminate or curtail in order to give more to God?

CHAPTER 6

Obedience—the Proof of Love

If anyone loves Me, he will keep My word . . . .
He who does not love Me does not keep My words . . . .

(John 14:23, 24)

Have you ever seen a crucified man's hands? I haven't, nor have I met anyone who has. But on the evening of the day He rose from the dead, Jesus made sure His disciples saw with their own eyes the nail prints in both His hands and His feet (Luke 24:39; John 20:20). He did this to prove that He lives. But those scars also prove that He loves.

> . . . and walk in love, just as Christ also loved you and gave Himself up for us, an offering and a sacrifice to God as a fragrant aroma (Ephesians 5:2; see John 15:13; 1 John 3:16).

Jesus had already demonstrated His love time and again by healing the sick, casting out demons, and showing compassion for the downtrodden and the rejects of society. But at the cross Jesus gave love its most dramatic and dynamic definition. More than anything else, the cross shows just how much God loves us. Jesus demonstrated love in its costliest, purest form. He gave His life for both friend and foe, Jew and Gentile, priest and prostitute— sinners all! What greater proof of love could He have given?

But if Jesus proved His love by dying for us, how can we prove our love for Him? We don't have to wonder. On the night before His hands and feet were pierced on our behalf, He revealed exactly what demonstrates our love for Him:

> If you love Me, you will keep My commandments (John 14:15).

> He who has My commandments and keeps them is the one who loves Me . . . (John 14:21).

If anyone loves Me, he will keep My word . . . (John 14:23).

You are My friends if you do what I command you (John 15:14).

Since He said it four times that evening, do you suppose He knew that His disciples (including us) needed to hear it more than once in order for the truth to sink in?

If Anyone Loves Me . . . .

Love and obedience naturally go together. "Love is the best motive to obedience, and obedience is the best proof of love."[81] Love and obedience can no more be separated from one another than faith and works (James 2:26). Disobedient love is an oxymoron; loveless obedience is only a shell. "As obedience is the essential consequence of love, so love is the essential basis of obedience."[82]

> I love Thee, I love Thee, and that Thou dost know;
> But how much I love Thee my actions will show.[83]

What God Most Wants

What does God most want from us? Isn't it a personal relationship with each of us? But sin—our sin—prevents fellowship with our holy God. If we are to have a relationship with Him, the sin barrier we erected must be removed so that we are no longer His enemies (Romans 5:8-11; 2 Corinthians 5:18-19). The problem is that even though we're the ones who put up this barrier, we have no power to take it down. Even if we never sinned again, which isn't going to happen, we could never cancel the huge backlog of sins already on our record. Nor could we do enough good works to balance the scales; it doesn't work that way. Neither can we pay for our own sins by laying down our lives. Without God's help we would remain helpless, hopeless sinners.

But here's where grace comes in. Instead of alienation, God offers reconciliation. Jesus' death bridges the yawning gap between God's holiness and our sinfulness. Jesus—divine and human, resident of both heaven and earth, sinless yet sin-bearer—reconciles us to our holy God in a wonderful new relationship we never had before and could never have had without Him. In Christ, God goes far beyond being our Creator and Provider—He becomes our Redeemer and Father. Only Jesus could accomplish this, and only by His cross is it possible.

"Love," says Merrill Tenney, "is the basis of our relationship with God. His love has been manifested in the gift of Jesus (1 John 4:9-10). Our love for him is expressed in obedience (1 John 5:3)."[84] In the words of Andrew Murray, "The secret of a true obedience . . . is the clear and close personal relationship to God."[85]

Pleasing Him

The perfect harmony Jesus enjoyed with His Father serves as a model for our relationship with God. On two separate occasions God announced His approval, "This is My beloved Son, in whom I am well-pleased" (Matthew 3:17; 17:5). What was there about Jesus that so pleased His Father? Jesus said, ". . . I always do the things that are pleasing to Him" (John 8:29). The Son's consistent obedience pleased His Father. And the motive for His obedience was love:

> . . . so that the world may know that I love the Father, I do exactly as the Father commanded Me (John 14:31).

According to what Jesus says here, how would the world know He loved the Father? How then can the world know we love the Father? ". . . we keep His commandments and do the things that are pleasing in His sight" (1 John 3:22).

As the following passages make clear, either we please God or we do not:

> . . . the mind set on the flesh is **hostile toward God**; for it does not subject itself to the law of God, for it is not even able to do

so, and those who are in the flesh **cannot please God** (Romans 8:7-8, emphasis added).

. . . as you received from us instruction as to **how you ought to walk and please God** (just as you actually do walk), that you excel still more (1 Thessalonians 4:1).

The second passage above proves that God is not impossible to please. The Thessalonian Christians pleased Him. How did they please Him? By doing His will. How did they know what His will was? Paul said, ". . . you received from us instruction as to how you ought to walk and please God . . . ." They had been taught, and then they put what they learned into practice. And that's exactly how we do it today. God's Word tells us how to please Him.

Jesus makes absolutely clear what the relationship of love and obedience is: "If anyone loves Me, he will keep My word . . . . He who does not love Me does not keep My words . . ." (John 14:23, 24). If we love Him, we will obey Him; if we don't love Him, we won't—it's that simple.

Pitfalls to Avoid

God desires for us to respond to His love by loving Him in return, and the way He wants us to demonstrate our love is by doing His will. His Word teaches us how to avoid the snares that hinder the loving obedience He desires. Here are five of those snares:

1) The Terror Trap

There is no fear in love; but perfect love casts out fear, because fear involves punishment, and the one who fears is not perfected in love (1 John 4:18).

Commenting on this passage, Frank Pack explains: "God could not be a God of justice and love without showing men the outcome of their disobedience to Him, but this is not the primary motive by which He appeals to us to live for Him and to serve Him."[86]

Citing 1 John 2:3-6, C. Michael Moss comments, "Children may obey their parents because they fear the consequence of not obeying. The sign of maturity is an obedient lifestyle that grows out of who the child is and the relationship developed with his or her parents. The same is true with regard to obedience toward God."[87]

2) The Legalism Trap

What God yearns for is a deeply personal fellowship with each of us (John 14:23; Acts 17:27; 2 Corinthians 6:16-18; Revelation 3:20). His commandments provide the framework for this fellowship. Love wants to please Him. Going through the motions of obedience without love cannot please Him. Loveless "obedience" is not obedience.

The only authentic faith is a working faith; the only genuine love is a love that labors (1 Thessalonians 1:3; James 2:14-26). As Leon Morris says, "In modern times love and obedience are often contrasted, obedience being connected with a legalistic spirit. But this antithesis is a false one. True love delights to obey (see 1 John 5:3). Those who know what love in the Christian sense really is are always eager to obey God's commandments." [88]

In the words of an unknown poet:

I will not work my soul to save,
For that my Lord has done;
But I will work like any slave,
For love of God's dear Son! [89]

God intends for love to be the driving force behind all our acts of obedience. The legalistic mindset cannot understand this. Invited by Simon the Pharisee into his home, Jesus tried to help him understand that the person who is forgiven most loves most (Luke 7:36-50). On that occasion, a sinful woman entered Simon's home and began pouring out her love for Christ by anointing His feet and wetting them with her tears. In contrast,

Simon had neglected giving to Jesus even the most common courtesies expected of a gracious host. Her act of service was how she expressed her gratitude and love for the forgiveness Jesus had shown her. This is what Simon failed to grasp.

Simon's self-righteousness blinded him to what another Pharisee, who later became the apostle Paul, came to realize:

> . . . I count all things to be loss in view of the surpassing value of knowing Christ Jesus my Lord, for whom I have suffered the loss of all things, and count them but rubbish so that I may gain Christ, and may be found in Him, **not having a righteousness of my own derived from the Law**, but that which is through faith in Christ, the righteousness which comes from God on the basis of faith, that I may know Him and the power of His resurrection and the fellowship of His sufferings, being conformed to His death; in order that I may attain to the resurrection from the dead (Philippians 3:8- 11, emphasis added).

Paul's relationship with Christ had provided him with an exciting new dimension he had never enjoyed as a Pharisee. Now he was totally focused on Jesus: knowing Him, gaining Him, being found in Him, identifying with His sufferings— even desiring to be conformed to His death. No longer was he attempting the impossible: attaining righteousness by keeping the law of Moses (Romans 3:20; Galatians 2:16). How could we possibly ever earn, deserve, or merit our salvation, no matter how much we do or how well we do it? Now that Paul had found the Messiah to whom Moses had pointed, he could then enjoy what so long had eluded him: a right relationship with God. Now he could not only learn how to live but also how to love.

3) The Reluctance Trap

Does God want us to serve Him with an unwilling spirit? No one feels good about receiving a gift offered out of a mere sense of obligation. "For the gift without the giver is bare."[90] But when a gift represents the genuine affection of the giver, then it pleases.

When Paul encouraged the Corinthians to contribute generously for their poor Jewish brethren, he said, "Each one must do just as he has purposed in his heart, not grudgingly or under compulsion, for God loves a cheerful giver" (2 Corinthians 9:7). Holding up the Macedonians as examples of giving liberally out of a sense of joy and privilege, Paul wrote, "I am not speaking this as a command, but as proving through the earnestness of others the sincerity of your love also" (2 Corinthians 8:8). If the Corinthians gave merely from a sense of obligation, what a blessing they would have forfeited!

Do our efforts to serve God lack the spontaneous joy that makes obedience such a blessing both to God and to ourselves? If so, we can learn from the apostle John how to have a different perspective: "For this is the love of God, that we keep His commandments; and His commandments are not burdensome" (1 John 5:3).

4) The Emotion Trap

Fear of hell and reluctance in serving both lack the fervent, heartfelt response God desires from us. But is it possible to go to the other extreme by seeking excitement without substance? What if getting goose bumps and "warm fuzzies" in worship means more to us than pleasing God? Is it possible that we have mistaken emotional highs for love of God?

Jesus said, "He who has My commandments and keeps them is the one who loves Me . . ." (John 14:21). Commenting on this verse, C. E. W. Dorris warned, "It is of the highest importance to us that we shall not overlook this pregnant utterance and substitute for obedience emotional ecstasies."[91]

First Corinthians 13 is famously known as the Love Chapter. What a gem! Yet, the most comprehensive treatment of love in the Bible is found in the little letter of 1 John. Here John uses the noun for love (*agapē*) 18 times, and the verb (*agapaō*) 25 times (excluding two references to a sinful love of the world). John speaks of God's love for us, our love for God, and our love (or lack of) for one another.

But what kind of love? As C. K. Barrett writes, "John never permits love to devolve into a sentiment or an emotion. Its expression is always moral and is revealed in obedience."[92] Or as David Lipscomb put it, "Love as presented by Jesus is not a mere sentiment, but it is a living, active principle." [93]

There's nothing wrong with goose bumps when we are deeply moved by the majesty and lovingkindness of God, but what God values most is that steady, day-in-and-day-out faithful love that gratefully seeks to please Him by simply doing what He said. This commitment to obedience will get us through those "dry times" when we don't feel especially stirred.

5) The Love-in-Word-Only Trap

How easy it is to profess love for God, but He knows whether our actions match our words, and if we are truly "obedient from the heart" (Romans 6:17). When we claim to love God but then don't act like it, how does that make Him feel?

The apostle of love bluntly wrote, "The one who says, 'I have come to know Him,' and does not keep His commandments, is a liar, and the truth is not in him . . ." (1 John 2:4; see Titus 1: 16). In other words, "If you have an obedience problem, you have a love problem." [94]

Frank Pack says it well:

> I am not driven to do God's will by the taskmaster's lash. I am driven by the compelling force of God's love for me. When I realize this sufficiently enough I am going to love Him deeply, and give my life to Him in service that demonstrates that love. I am going to find that the deepest hurt I have is when I hurt Him through my indifference and sinfulness. I will feel a hungering and thirsting after righteousness that describes the kind of life He wants me to live.[95]

God has been far too good to us for us to return evil for good.

All He wants from us is that we love, trust, and obey Him. Is that asking too much?

So What Does It Mean to be Saved by Grace?

J. I. Packer writes: "The grace of God is love freely shown towards guilty sinners, contrary to their merit and indeed in defiance of their demerit. It is God showing goodness to persons who deserve only severity, and no reason to expect anything but severity." [96]

How could we possibly ever earn, deserve, or merit the salvation God offers us so freely by His grace? That's exactly the point Paul makes in two of his letters, as the following chart shows. It is remarkable the way both passages follow the same pattern and make the same points, often using the same vocabulary:

The Three Stages	Ephesians 2:1-10	Titus 3:3-8
Before Conversion	And you were dead in your trespasses and sins, in which you formerly walked according to the course of this world, according to the prince of the power of the air, of the spirit that is now working in the sons of *disobedience*. Among them we too all formerly lived in the *lusts* of our flesh, indulging the desires of the flesh and of the mind, and were by nature children of wrath, even as the rest.	For we also once were foolish ourselves, *disobedient*, deceived, enslaved to various *lusts* and pleasures, spending our life in malice and envy, hateful, hating one another.

The Three Stages	Ephesians 2:1-10	Titus 3:3-8
How God Saves Us and How He Does *Not* Save Us	But God, being rich in **mercy**, because of His great **love** [*agapē*] with which He **loved** [*agapaō*] us, even when we were dead in our transgressions, made us alive together with Christ (by **grace** you have been *saved*), and raised us up with Him, and seated us with Him in the heavenly places in Christ Jesus, so that in the ages to come He might show the surpassing riches of His **grace** in **kindness** toward us in Christ Jesus. For by **grace** you have been saved through faith; and that not of yourselves, it is the gift of God; *not as a result of works, so that no one may boast.*	But when the **kindness** of God our Savior and His **love for mankind** [*philanthrōpia*] appeared, He saved us, *not on the basis of deeds which we have done in righteousness,* but according to His **mercy**, by the washing of regeneration and renewing by the Holy Spirit, whom He poured out upon us richly through Jesus Christ our Savior, so that being justified by His **grace** we would be made heirs according to the hope of eternal life.
After Conversion	For we are His workmanship, created in Christ Jesus for *good works*, which God prepared beforehand so that we would walk in them.	This is a trustworthy statement; and concerning these things I want you to speak confidently, so that those who have believed God will be careful to engage in *good deeds*. These things are good and profitable for men.

It has been rightly said that the Bible is its own best interpreter. Paul's letter to Titus helps us understand what he says to the Ephesians. From the previous chart, let's focus on these verses in particular:

Ephesians 2:8-9	Titus 3:5
For by grace you have been saved through faith; and that not of yourselves, it is the gift of God; not as a result of works, so that no one may boast.	. . . He saved us, not on the basis of deeds which we have done in righteousness, but according to His mercy, by the washing of regeneration and renewing by the Holy Spirit . . . .

In Ephesians, Paul says we are saved by grace through faith, not of works. What kind of works? Those we might be tempted to boast about, Paul says. Applying good common sense to the question of grace and works, F. LaGard Smith offers this illustration:

> . . . suppose a man is drowning in turbulent waters and a bystander throws him a life-preserver which lands well within his reach. If the man grabs hold of the life-preserver, he will be saved. If he does not, he will drown. At this point, it's all up to him. Grab or not grab. Be saved or be lost. What will it be?

> If our drowning man reaches out and grabs hold of the lifepreserver and is saved, would anyone dare suggest that he merits being saved simply for having grasped the preserver? Or that he "worked" for his safe deliverance from peril?

> Here's a good test: Do you think our rescued man is going to go around boasting to all his friends about how valiantly he saved himself, or is he more likely to tell them about the person who came along and threw him the life-preserver? Is he going to take credit for his own heroism, or keep asking his rescuer, "What can I do to show appreciation for what you've done?"[97]

In his letter to Titus, Paul clarifies that although we are not saved by "deeds which we have done in righteousness," we *are* saved "by the washing of regeneration and renewing by the Holy Spirit." Eminent church historian Everett Ferguson comments:

To my knowledge early Christian writers never referred the "washing of regeneration" of Titus 3:5 to anything other than baptism. I have consulted the references to Titus 3:5 in Biblica Patristica up to the fourth century and selectively after that. All writers that comment on the meaning, beginning with Theophilus, bishop of Antioch in the late second century, identify the washing (or bath) of regeneration as water baptism . . . . Epiphanius, bishop of Salamis in the fourth century sums up the general understanding succinctly, "the washing of regeneration is the baptism of water" (Panarion 9.4.8).[98]

Note that in the Titus passage Paul does not classify baptism in the category of "deeds which we have done in righteousness"—which cannot save. Paul himself had once been commanded by Ananias, "Now why do you delay? Get up and be baptized, and wash away your sins, calling on His name" (Acts 22:16). Christ Himself had sent Ananias to tell him this. Paul obeyed (Acts 9:18). Even though Paul had already seen Christ on the road to Damascus and for the first time had come to believe in Him, and even though he had just spent three days in fasting and prayer—obviously penitent (Acts 9:9, 11), he still had sins to wash away! Although he was certainly moving in the right direction, he was not yet a saved man. Even though faith in Jesus and a penitent heart were absolutely essential to his salvation, they were not sufficient in themselves to bring about the cleansing he so desperately needed. His newfound faith and sincere repentance prepared his heart for what he still lacked: being united with Christ in baptism (Romans 6:3-5; Galatians 3:27).

And so Ananias told him, "Get up and be baptized, and wash away your sins . . . ." What washed away Paul's sins? Certainly not the water, but rather the blood of Christ (Matthew 26:28; Romans 5:9; Hebrews 9:12, 14; 10:29; Revelation 1:5). And His blood still cleanses whenever we unite with Him as we are baptized into His death, burial, and resurrection (Colossians 2:12-13). Cleansing by the blood of Christ must occur at some point. Titus 3:5 and other passages identify that point as "the washing of regeneration."

Some use the Ephesian passage in the aforementioned chart in an attempt to prove that baptism is not essential to salvation, since it says that we are not saved by works. Here again, the Bible is its own best interpreter. Francis Foulkes says, "Without fear of contradiction it may be said that there are more numerous and more sustained similarities between Ephesians and Colossians than between any other two New Testament epistles."[99] So what light does Colossians shed on Ephesians?

Ephesians 2:4-6	Colossians 2:12-13
But God, being rich in mercy, because of His great love with which He loved us, even when we were **dead in our transgressions,** *made us alive together with Christ* (by grace you have been saved), and **raised us up with Him,** and seated us with Him in the heavenly places in Christ Jesus	. . . having been buried with Him in baptism, in which you were also **raised up with Him** through faith in the working of God, who raised Him from the dead. When you were **dead in your transgressions** and the uncircumcision of your flesh, *He made you alive together with Him,* having forgiven us all our transgressions . . . .

Both passages speak of 1) being dead in sin, 2) being raised up with Christ, and 3) being made alive with Him. Colossians clarifies what is meant by being raised up with Him: this happens in baptism. Note these contrasts in the Colossian passage:

BURIED with Him in baptism . . . RAISED up with Him
DEAD in your transgressions . . . ALIVE together with Him

FORGIVEN!

And After Baptism?

The Christians at Thessalonica were among those who had experienced God's grace. They had "turned to God from idols to serve a living and true God, and to wait for His Son from heaven . . ." (1 Thessalonians 1:9-10). Once they had made that radical change of mindset and lifestyle, Paul could commend them for their "work of faith and labor of love" (1 Thessalonians 1:3; see James 2:14-26). They were now practicing what should always follow conversion—they were "careful to engage in good deeds" (Titus 3:8). Sad to say, many Christians apparently don't understand that good works must follow conversion. As Leslie G. Thomas writes, "Inactivity in the Lord's work is one of the worst things which can happen to a child of God."[100] And Delmar Owens agrees: "Wasted manpower in God's church is one of the saddest spectacles of our time. Some church members are like the lilies—'they toil not, neither do they spin.'"[101]

The Benefits of Love

"Loving Christ pays unmatched benefits," says Merrill Tenney.[102] What are those benefits?

1) The first is having the love and fellowship of the Father and the Son:

> He who has My commandments and keeps them is the one who loves Me; and he who loves Me will be loved by My Father, and I will love him and will disclose Myself to him . . . . If anyone loves Me, he will keep My word; and My Father will love him, and We will come to him and make Our abode with him (John 14:21, 23).

> If you keep My commandments, you will abide in My love; just as I have kept My Father's commandments and abide in His love (John 15:10).

2) Another benefit is having the assurance that we have come to know Him:

By this we know that we have come to know Him, if we keep His commandments. The one who says, "I have come to know Him," and does not keep His commandments, is a liar, and the truth is not in him; but whoever keeps His word, in him the love of God has truly been perfected. By this we know that we are in Him: the one who says he abides in Him ought himself to walk in the same manner as He walked (1 John 2:3-6).

3) A third benefit is having God grant our prayers (the subject of our next chapter):

Beloved, if our heart does not condemn us, we have confidence before God; and whatever we ask we receive from Him, because we keep His commandments and do the things that are pleasing in His sight (1 John 3:21-22).

These are only three of the many good things that come our way when we live God's way and reflect His love. God pleads with us to love and obey Him, not only to make fellowship with Him possible, but also because He knows that loving obedience will bring us the greatest blessings. The happiest people in the world are those who have discovered these truths and made them real in their own lives.

Are we among them?

Questions:

1. Review the five traps discussed above.
2. Review the three benefits of love.
3. It has been said that Jesus never asks of us what He Himself was unwilling to do. How does Jesus serve as our model of love and obedience?
4. Why does God have such a strong desire for a personal relationship with each of us that He was willing to pay such a costly price to make reconciliation possible?

5. Why is love so commonly misunderstood?

6. Why is there such a strong de-emphasis today on baptism?

CHAPTER 7

God Listens If We Will

For the eyes of the LORD are toward the righteous,
And His ears attend to their prayer,
But the face of the LORD is against those who do evil.

(1 Peter 3:12)

For awhile after 9-11, "God Bless America" was all over the place—on bumper stickers and even on signs in front of businesses. Was America finally turning back to God? Was this the long-overdue turnaround our country so desperately needed?

How much lasting change has resulted from the trauma of that dreadful day in September? Or have we as a nation largely "recovered" from our suddenly-heightened spiritual awareness?

My doctor commented to me, "Why should God bless America?" It disturbed him that so many in our nation after 9-11 cried out for God's blessing without that corresponding change of heart that God requires. He had a point. True repentance results in changed lives (Luke 3:7-14; Acts 26:19-20). When I told him I had seen a bumper sticker that said, "America Bless God," he wanted to know where he could get one. What will it take for a truly heart-changing revival to break out in our beloved land?

The good news is that we serve a prayer-hearing God (Psalm 65:2). God cares so much about His children that He wants to hear from them—often. And since we have in Jesus a sympathetic and able high priest who intercedes with the Father on our behalf, "let us draw near with confidence to the throne of grace, so that we may receive mercy and find grace to help in time of need" (Hebrews 4:16).

But does everyone who prays to God receive a favorable hearing? If not, who has God's ear? To what extent does the way we live affect God's willingness to hear our prayers? What does God expect of us? Would God be more inclined to listen if we made some changes?

Whose Prayer Will God Hear?

It's impressive how often this principle is found in both the Old and New Testaments. It is sometimes stated positively, sometimes negatively. And it is applied to a wide variety of situations. For example:

If I regard wickedness in my heart,
The Lord will not hear (Psalm 66:18).

Because he has loved Me, therefore I will deliver him;
I will set him securely on high, because he has known My name.
He will call upon Me, and I will answer him . . . (Psalm 91:14-15a).

The LORD is near to all who call upon Him,
To all who call upon Him in truth.
He will fulfill the desire of those who fear Him;
He will also hear their cry and will save them (Psalm 145:18-19).

The sacrifice of the wicked is an abomination to the LORD,
But the prayer of the upright is His delight (Proverbs 15:8).

The LORD is far from the wicked,
But He hears the prayer of the righteous (Proverbs 15:29).

He who shuts his ear to the cry of the poor
Will also cry himself and not be answered (Proverbs 21:13).

He who turns away his ear from listening to the law,
Even his prayer is an abomination (Proverbs 28:9).

"Why have we fasted and You do not see?
Why have we humbled ourselves and You do not notice?"
Behold, on the day of your fast you find your desire,
And drive hard all your workers.
Behold, you fast for contention and strife and to strike with a
   wicked fist.
You do not fast like you do today to make your voice heard on
high (Isaiah 58:3-4; see 1:15).

Is this not the fast which I choose,
To loosen the bonds of wickedness,

To undo the bands of the yoke,
And to let the oppressed go free
And break every yoke?
Is it not to divide your bread with the hungry
And bring the homeless poor into the house;
When you see the naked, to cover him;
And not to hide yourself from your own flesh?
Then your light will break out like the dawn,
And your recovery will speedily spring forth;
And your righteousness will go before you;
The glory of the LORD will be your rear guard.
Then you will call, and the LORD will answer;
You will cry, and He will say, "Here I am" (Isaiah 58:6-9).

Behold, the LORD'S hand is not so short
That it cannot save;
Nor is His ear so dull
That it cannot hear.
But your iniquities have made a separation between you and your
    God,
And your sins have hidden His face from you so that He does not
    hear (Isaiah 59:1-2—see the remainder of the chapter).

"And now, because you [the people of Judah] have done all these things," declares the LORD, "and I spoke to you, rising up early and speaking, but you did not hear, and I called you but you did not answer . . . . As for you [Jeremiah], do not pray for this people, and do not lift up cry or prayer for them, and do not intercede with Me; for I do not hear you" (Jeremiah 7:13, 16).

They have turned back to the iniquities of their ancestors who refused to hear My words, and they have gone after other gods to serve them . . . . though they will cry to Me, yet I will not listen to them (Jeremiah 11:10-11; see 14:10-12).

We have transgressed and rebelled,
You have not pardoned.
You have covered Yourself with anger
And pursued us;
You have slain and have not spared.

You have covered Yourself with a cloud
So that no prayer can pass through (Lamentations 3:42-44).

Is it too light a thing for the house of Judah to commit the abominations which they have committed here, that they have filled the land with violence and provoked Me repeatedly? . . . . though they cry in My ears with a loud voice, yet I will not listen to them (Ezekiel 8:17-18).

Then they will cry out to the LORD,
But He will not answer them.
Instead, He will hide His face from them at that time
Because they have practiced evil deeds (Micah 3:4).

"But they refused to pay attention and turned a stubborn shoulder and stopped their ears from hearing. They made their hearts like flint so that they could not hear the law and the words which the LORD of hosts had sent by His Spirit through the former prophets; therefore great wrath came from the LORD of hosts. And just as He called and they would not listen, so they called and I would not listen," says the LORD of hosts . . . (Zechariah 7:11-13).

You ask and do not receive, because you ask with wrong motives, so that you may spend it on your pleasures. You adulteresses, do you not know that friendship with the world is hostility toward God? Therefore whoever wishes to be a friend of the world makes himself an enemy of God (James 4:3-4).

You husbands in the same way, live with your wives in an understanding way, as with someone weaker, since she is a woman; and show her honor as a fellow heir of the grace of life, so that your prayers will not be hindered (1 Peter 3:7; see Malachi 2:13-16).

. . . and whatever we ask we receive from Him, because we keep His commandments and do the things that are pleasing in His sight (1 John 3:22).

"One of the most thrilling passages in all the Bible" is how Mack Lyon describes the last verse cited above.[103] Regarding this passage, R. A. Torrey has written:

I was once speaking to a woman who had been a professed Christian, but had given it all up. I asked her why she was not a Christian still. She replied, because she did not believe the Bible. I asked her why she did not believe the Bible.

"Because I have tried its promises and found them untrue."

"Which promises?"

"The promises about prayer."

"Which promises about prayer?"

"Does it not say in the Bible, 'Whatsoever ye ask believing ye shall receive'?"

"It says something nearly like that."

"Well, I have asked fully expecting to get and did not receive, so the promise failed."

"Was the promise made to you?"

"Why, certainly, it is made to all Christians, is it not?"

"No, God carefully defines . . . whose believing prayers He agrees to answer."

I then turned her to 1 John 3:22, and read the description of those whose prayers had power with God.

"Now," I said, "were you keeping His commandments and doing those things which are pleasing in His sight?"

She frankly confessed that she was not, and soon came to see that the real difficulty was not with God's promises, but with herself. That is the difficulty with many an unanswered prayer today: the one who offers it is not obedient.[104]

Time to Take Inventory

Looking again at the passages cited above, as shown in the following chart, let's each examine ourselves and ask: On which side of the ledger am I?

Passage	Whose Prayer Will God *Not* Hear?	Whose Prayer *Will* God Hear?
Psalm 66:18	he who regards wickedness in his heart	
Psalm 91:14-15		the one who loves God and knows His name
Psalm 145:18-19		those who call upon God in truth, those who fear Him
Proverbs 15:8, 29	the wicked	the upright, the righteous
Proverbs 21:13	he who shuts his ear to the cry of the poor	
Proverbs 28:9	he who turns away his ear from listening to the law	
Isaiah 58:3-9	those who oppress others	those who end oppression and who provide for the needy
Isaiah 59:1ff.	those who sin but do not repent	
Jeremiah 7:13, 16	those who do not hear God	
Jeremiah 11:10-11	idolaters	
Lamentations 3:42-44	those who have transgressed and rebelled	
Ezekiel 8:17-18	those who commit abominations/violence	
Micah 3:4	those who practice evil deeds	
Zechariah 7:11-13	those who refuse to listen to the law or the prophets	
James 4:3-4	those who ask with wrong motives and are friends of the world	
1 Peter 3:7	those who do not live considerately with their wives	
1 Peter 3:12	those who do evil	the righteous
1 John 3:22		those who obey God and do what pleases Him

Commenting on 1 Peter 3:7 above, Charles Bigg says, ". . . the sighs of the injured wife come between the husband's prayer and God's hearing . . . ."[105] For those of us who are married, that should give us something to think about!

Additional passages could be cited.[106] But these should be sufficient to make the point: God will not hear us if we persist in sin. As Torrey wrote, "Sin is an awful thing, and one of the most awful things about it is the way it hinders prayer, the way it severs the connection between us and the source of all grace and power and blessing. Any one who would have power in prayer must be merciless in dealing with his own sins."[107]

But God is open to our prayers if we listen to His Word and obey Him. Our prayer life cannot be separated from all of life. Mack Lyon offers these painfully soul-searching observations:

> Most assuredly there are some in the church whose prayers are so profitless they are inclined to give it up as weariness and mockery, for this very reason—they do not keep the commandments of the Lord and they refuse to do the things that are pleasing in His sight. To be practical, the person who professes a love of God in prayer, but forsakes the assemblies of God's people for worship in disobedience to Hebrews 10:25, will find his prayers abomination—not only before God, but also in his own estimation.[108]

James Tolle writes, ". . . many Christians live spiritually indolent, impure lives and expect the mouthing of a few words of prayer from time to time to make all things right between themselves and their Creator. Needless to say, they pray in vain. It is impossible to graft righteous prayer on a slippery life."[109]

So the Scriptures are quite clear: God listens to those who listen to Him, but He won't hear those whose ears are closed to Him. Doesn't that make perfectly good sense? Why should it be any other way?

Biblical Case Studies

Not only does the Bible repeatedly state the principle, but it also provides us with many examples of individuals who either did or did not have God's ear when they prayed. Let's consider two by way of contrast.

An Avoidable Tragedy

What potential King Saul had! Initially he enjoyed the favor of his people and displayed courageous leadership. But due to his self-willed disobedience to clear commands from God, he met his downfall (1 Samuel 13, 15; 1 Chronicles 10:13). As a result, God withdrew His Spirit from Saul, transferred the kingship to David, and refused to answer when Saul sought God's guidance (1 Samuel 14:37; 28:6). The night before his death, Saul despaired, ". . . God has departed from me and no longer answers me, either through prophets or by dreams . . ." (1 Samuel 28:15). This pathetic breach between Saul and God could have been avoided if he had learned early to listen (1 Chronicles 10:13-14).

The Man Whom God Esteemed

In stark contrast to Saul is the prophet Daniel. Taken by force from his homeland and transported with other captives several hundred miles east to what is present-day Iraq, Daniel found himself in a totally alien culture. Not only were the Babylonian language and customs different from his Judean upbringing, but pagan values prevailed. When social expectations demanded conformity, Daniel refused to compromise his convictions (Daniel 1:3-16). In his service to the king he demonstrated such absolute integrity that his enemies "could find no ground of accusation or evidence of corruption, inasmuch as he was faithful, and no negligence or corruption was to be found in him" (Daniel 6:4). (Oh, that this could more often be said today of those who hold political office!)

When prayer to anyone but the king became illegal, Daniel kept prayers to his God ascending, just as always, resulting in his being thrown into the den of lions. God preserved his life. On a later occasion, in response to Daniel's earnest prayer, God sent the angel Gabriel with this message: "At the beginning of your supplications the command was issued, and I have come to tell you, for you are highly esteemed . . ." (Daniel 9:23). What a compliment—"you are highly esteemed"—and from no less than God Himself! As Andrew Murray has written, "The life speaks louder and truer than the lips. To pray well I must live well. He who seeks to live with God will learn to know His mind and to please Him, so that he will be able to pray according to His will."[110]

Daniel had his set times for prayer (Daniel 6:10), but this was no empty ritual. As Murray said, "To pray well I must live well." Because Daniel lived well, he prayed well—and God heard him.

The Two Contrasted

"I regret that I have made Saul king," God told Samuel, "for he has turned back from following Me and has not carried out My commands" (1 Samuel 15:11). One of the saddest verses in the Bible says, "Now the Spirit of the LORD departed from Saul, and an evil spirit from the LORD terrorized him" (1 Samuel 16:14). Forsaken by God and desperate for answers, Saul violated God's law by consulting a medium to bring up the departed spirit of Samuel. When he appeared, Saul asked him for guidance. Samuel asked, "Why then do you ask me, since the LORD has departed from you and has become your adversary?" (1 Samuel 28:16). Imagine, having God for an enemy!

But God had a totally different relationship with Daniel. He sent Gabriel to say, "O Daniel, man of high esteem . . . . from the first day that you set your heart on understanding this and on humbling yourself before your God, your words were heard, and I have come in response to your words" (Daniel 10:11-12). *Powerful!*

The Principle in Our Day

Really, nothing has changed. There are still self-directed people like Saul and obedient people like Daniel. God turns a deaf ear to the one and eagerly listens to the other. As Joe Barnett has written,

> I have a friend who is often depressed. He complains that God doesn't give him the breaks, doesn't answer his prayers. "God doesn't seem to be listening to me," he says.
>
> I really don't know why God should listen to him. He certainly doesn't seem to be listening to God. He's not a generous giver—not a soul winner—not a consistent Bible reader—not a regular worshipper. But when he gets into a predicament and calls on God for help, he feels God should drop everything and bail him out. I thought another friend answered him pretty well. When he whined, "Why doesn't God hear my prayers?" he answered, "Maybe God is busy taking care of His regular customers."[111]

Through the years I have looked at the table of contents of various books on prayer. It's noteworthy how many of these books have a chapter on "hindrances to prayer." In one such book, E. M. Bounds refers to what Jesus taught about going into one's closet, as the King James Version phrases it, for private one-on-One with our Father who sees in secret (Matthew 6:5-6):

> John said of primitive Christian praying, "Whatsoever we ask we receive of him, because we keep his commandments and do those things which are pleasing in his sight" . . . . Their lives were not only true and obedient, but they were thinking about things above obedience, searching for and doing things to make God glad. These can come with eager step and radiant countenance to meet their Father in the closet, not simply to be forgiven, but to be approved and to receive.[112]

The Other Side of the Coin

Does God hear sinners when they pray? Often when this question is asked, the following verse is quoted: "We know that God does not hear sinners; but if anyone is God-fearing and does His will,

He hears him" (John 9:31). This was said by a man Jesus had just healed of blindness. The Pharisees who were grilling the man about his relationship to Jesus would no doubt have agreed with his statement about whose prayer God would hear. Where the Pharisees and the former blind man parted company was focused on the issue of how to classify Jesus—whether a sinner or a God-fearing, obedient man.

"We know that God does not hear sinners . . . ." One of my teachers observed that the one who said this, the former blind man, was not speaking by inspiration. Though that is true, he was nevertheless speaking a biblical truth, reflecting many of the passages cited in the first part of this chapter. Simply stated, the principle is: If we listen to God, He will listen to us; if we do not listen, He will not hear us. The man whose eyes Jesus opened was simply stating an axiomatic truth, a given.

But the discussion of whether God will hear a sinner's prayer is not complete without looking at the conversion of Cornelius, the first Gentile to become a Christian. Before he heard the gospel, an angel appeared to him while he was praying and told him, "Cornelius, your prayer has been heard and your alms have been remembered before God" (Acts 10:31; see 10:4).

Did Cornelius pray the so-called "sinner's prayer" we hear so much about today? In other words, did his prayer of faith save him the very moment he prayed? What did the angel tell him? "Send to Joppa and have Simon, who is also called Peter, brought here; *and he will speak words to you by which you will be saved, you and all your household*" (Acts 11:13-14, italics added). Was this devout man not yet saved? For all his devotion to God as expressed in his prayers and gifts to the poor, Cornelius was among those of whom Paul wrote, ". . . for all have sinned and fall short of the glory of God . . ." (Romans 3:23), and ". . . the wages of sin is death . . ." (Romans 6:23a). To be saved, Cornelius still needed to hear and obey the gospel. God knew the man's heart, and He knew Cornelius would obey if he only understood what to do. This is where Peter comes in. When Cornelius, along with his family and friends, heard Peter preach, they obeyed what they heard and were saved. But they remained unsaved until they had heard and responded to the gospel.

The case of Cornelius clarifies that the principle, "God does not hear sinners," refers to those who have no intention of repenting and obeying. Although God does not hear the prayer of those who resist His will, He saw in Cornelius an entirely different spirit. Though Cornelius was not saved until he was baptized (Acts 2:37-38, 41; 22:16), and he was not saved simply by praying, his prayers did help him move closer to the salvation that is in Christ alone. He was open to God, and so God was open to him. Before he heard and obeyed the gospel, he was like the man Jesus complimented who was "not far from the kingdom of God" (Mark 12:34). Not far, but not yet in.

I'd like to think that around the world at this moment there are many like Cornelius—men and women who truly want to obey God and are practicing all of God's will that they know. But they need more. From a human perspective they are good people, but they lack that righteousness, which can be found only in Christ. How precious they are to God! But they are still in their sins. Jesus died for them, but His blood has not yet been applied to their souls. Only in obedience to the gospel is anyone saved (2 Thessalonians 1:7-10; Hebrews 5:8-9; 1 Peter 4:17). But to obey, sinners must hear the gospel to know what God expects of them (Romans 10:13-17). And so for sincere seekers like Cornelius, all they need is for someone to tell them.

Questions:

1. "If I regard wickedness in my heart, the Lord will not hear" (Psalm 66:18). What does it mean to "regard wickedness in my

heart"? What could be some ways we might do this?

2. What can we do to maintain a vibrant prayer life even after a crisis passes?

3. Does God owe us anything?

4. Does a denial of a prayer request necessarily mean that our hearts are not right with God? Explain.

5. Why should we trust God in spite of His apparent slowness in responding to our prayers or when He seems indifferent to our needs?

6. Since it is hard to see ourselves objectively, how can we discover if there is something in our lives that may be hindering our prayers?

CHAPTER 8

Losing to Gain

**For whoever wishes to save his life will lose it;
but whoever loses his life for My sake will find it.**

(Matthew 16:25)

It was the discovery of a lifetime—what many dream of but few ever experience: hidden treasure! But there was just one hitch: Someone else owned the field where the treasure was stashed. The man who found it would never be satisfied until he had the deed to this property—and the treasure—in his hands. But to raise the needed capital he would have to liquidate all his assets—everything he owned. But he didn't mind one bit. He knew that what he gave up couldn't compare with what he would obtain! In "losing" he would gain, and he was glad (Matthew 13:44).

We may never stumble across hidden treasure, but in everyday life don't we operate on the principle of losing-to-gain? When we make up our minds to get an education, buy a house, or fund our retirement, aren't we willing to do what it takes to make it happen? That's why businesses invest such big bucks in advertising, research, and development. They're looking to turn a profit. CEOs don't bemoan the cost if they're convinced it's worth it. They know that success comes at a price, but it's a price they're willing to pay.

What is true of financial investments is just as true in the spiritual realm. Jesus' principle, quoted beneath the title of this chapter, is a paradox, defined by Webster's as "a statement that is seemingly contradictory or opposed to common sense and yet is perhaps true." [113] Since Jesus said it, in this case there is no "perhaps" about it. It is a certain truth with no exceptions. On the surface it may seem contradictory and nonsensical, but is true nonetheless, as further study makes clear.

Jesus stated this paradoxical principle on at least four separate occasions, as recorded in Matthew, Mark, Luke, and John. The wording varies slightly, but the basic thought remains the same. A comparison of these four variations can give us a clearer picture of what losing and saving one's life truly means:

Matthew 10:39	He who has found his life	will lose it	He who has lost his life for My sake	will find it.
Mark 8:35	Whoever wishes to save his life	will lose it	Whoever loses his life for My sake and the gospel's	will save it
Luke 17:33	Whoever seeks to keep his life	will lose it	Whoever loses his life	will preserve it.
John 12:25	He who loves his life	loses it	He who hates his life in this world	will keep it to life eternal

A blend of these passages could be paraphrased like this: Whoever loves his life in this world and seeks to preserve it will end up losing his life; but whoever hates his life in this world and is willing to lose it for My sake and the gospel's will keep it to eternal life.

In view of Jesus' principle, the old saying, "Finders, keepers; losers, weepers," could be re-phrased: "Keepers, losers; losers, finders." This principle is somewhat like the adage, "You can't have your cake and eat it too." We can't have it both ways. It is not both/and, but either/or. So we must choose.

The Principle in Context
Examining each of Jesus' four statements of this principle in context can help us understand better what He meant by losing to gain.

The Principle According to the Gospel of Matthew

In Matthew 10 Jesus sent out the apostles to preach and heal. Preparing them to face persecution, He drew two pairs of contrasts: whom to fear/whom not to fear, and confessing Christ/denying Christ:

> Do not fear those who kill the body but are unable to kill the soul; but rather fear Him who is able to destroy both soul and body in hell. Are not two sparrows sold for a cent? And yet not one of them will fall to the ground apart from your Father. But the very hairs of your head are all numbered. So do not fear; you are more valuable than many sparrows (Matthew 10:28-31).

> Therefore everyone who confesses Me before men, I will also confess him before My Father who is in heaven. But whoever denies Me before men, I will also deny him before My Father who is in heaven (Matthew 10:32-33).

The apostles would be tempted to deny Christ to save their skins, as Peter would later do. But if they would dare to confess Christ and take the consequences, they would have Christ's approval. Wouldn't it be worth the sacrifice?

What a blessing it is to live under a government that pledges itself to "ensure domestic tranquility," as the preamble to the U. S. Constitution puts it. But if the time should come, and it apparently is coming, that we cannot practice our faith without governmental interference, then we will be faced with the choice of whether to save our lives or lose them for Christ's sake and the gospel's.

Jesus warned them of the fierce opposition that could come even from family:

> Brother will betray brother to death, and a father his child; and children will rise up against parents and cause them to be put to death. You will be hated by all because of My name, but it is the one who has endured to the end who will be saved (Matthew 10:21-22).

. . . a man's enemies will be the members of his household. He who loves father or mother more than Me is not worthy of Me; and he who loves son or daughter more than Me is not worthy of Me. And he who does not take his cross and follow after Me is not worthy of Me. **He who has found his life will lose it, and he who has lost his life for My sake will find it** (Matthew 10:36-39, emphasis added).

How wonderful it is when everyone in the family is loyal to Christ, but when loved ones are hostile to Christ, the disciple is forced to choose between them and Him (Matthew 10:34-36). In such cases it is impossible to maintain a relationship with both family and Christ at the same time. One must choose.

Our natural desire for peace in the family (Matthew 10:21-22, 34-37) and for physical safety (Matthew 10:17, 28) must not take precedence over loyalty to the One who was willing to forfeit both for our sake. If we preserve our lives by denying Christ, we will be the ultimate losers. But if we lose our life because we have confessed Him, we will discover true life indeed. Being saved in the end (Matthew 10:22) is the equivalent to finding life (Matthew 10:39). And we will be like our Master. Paul, who understood this principle well, longed to experience "the fellowship of His sufferings, being conformed to His death; in order that I may attain to the resurrection from the dead" (Philippians 3:10-11; see 2:17; Hebrews 11:35). Paul was eager to forfeit his earthly life to gain the heavenly. And like the man who sold all to obtain the treasure, Paul was convinced it was well worth it (Romans 8:18; 2 Corinthians 4:17). He could say with conviction:

But whatever things were gain to me, those things I have counted as loss for the sake of Christ. More than that, I count all things to be loss in view of the surpassing value of knowing Christ Jesus my Lord, for whom I have suffered the loss of all things, and count them but rubbish so that I may gain Christ . . . (Philippians 3:7-8).

One cannot help but admire Paul's sacrificial spirit, as also exemplified by those who "did not love their life even when faced with death" (Revelation 12:11). Do we share their attitude?

But losing one's life for Christ's sake does not always mean martyrdom. Although we must be willing to lay down our lives for Christ, few of us will ever be called on to do so. Each of us, however, will face situations where it is easier to go along to get along. What then?

The Principle According to the Gospel of Mark

Jesus asked His disciples two questions. The first was easy to answer: "Who do people say that I am?" (Mark 8:27). To answer this question, all the disciples had to do was simply to report what they'd been hearing—that some thought Jesus was John the Baptist or a prophet from Israel's past. But Jesus' second question was of a different character altogether, one that required reflection and personal commitment: "But who do you say that I am?" (v. 29). When Peter then confessed Jesus as the Christ, he not only gave the correct answer, but he showed where he stood about Jesus. The Jewish leaders certainly did not share Peter's conviction. They would never say what Peter said.

Then Jesus steered the conversation in a most unwelcome direction: "And He began to teach them that the Son of Man must suffer many things and be rejected by the elders and the chief priests and the scribes, and be killed, and after three days rise again" (v. 31). This was too much for Peter: "God forbid it, Lord! This shall never happen to You" (Matthew 16:22). Peter's strong negative reaction to this announcement indicates that this was the first time Jesus had spoken directly of His death. When Peter took Jesus to task for speaking this way, his rebuke was met with an even stronger counter-rebuke: "Get behind Me, Satan!" Jesus said, "You are a stumbling block to Me; for you are not setting your mind on God's interests, but man's" (v. 23).

Why such an impassioned reaction from Peter when Jesus spoke of His impending death? Perhaps he could not bear the thought of seeing his beloved Master die. Or maybe the concept of a rejected Messiah seemed to Peter like a contradiction in terms. Or could it be that following Jesus had taken on a dangerous new turn for Peter personally? Would Peter himself also be killed along with His Lord? Whatever it was that Peter found so repugnant about Jesus' dying, he was on the wrong side of things, Jesus said.

Jesus then introduced the same principle He had already taught the apostles on an earlier occasion:

> If anyone wishes to come after Me, he must deny himself and take up his cross and follow Me. **For whoever wishes to save his life will lose it, but whoever loses his life for My sake and the gospel's will save it.** For what does it profit a man to gain the whole world and forfeit his soul? . . . . For whoever is ashamed of Me and My words in this adulterous and sinful generation, the Son of Man will also be ashamed of him when He comes in the glory of His Father with the holy angels (Mark 8:34-36, 38, emphasis added).

In announcing that He will suffer, be rejected and killed, but then rise again (v. 31), Jesus Himself models the principle: He will lose His life; He will gain His life. This helps us understand what He meant when He said, "If anyone wishes to come after Me, he must deny himself, and take up his cross and follow Me" (Mark 8:34). Taking up one's cross can certainly include martyrdom, and that's what it meant for most of the apostles, tradition tells us. But in Luke's account of this incident Jesus said, "If anyone wishes to come after Me, he must deny himself, and take up his cross *daily* and follow Me" (Luke 9:23, italics added). As D. A. Carson says, "'Taking one's cross' does not mean putting up with some awkward or tragic situation in one's life but painfully dying to self. In that sense every disciple of Jesus bears the same cross."[114] Larry Deason said it well: "The grip of selfishness is so strong in our hearts that we must begin by decisively rejecting it as a life principle. We cannot pick up the cross of Christ if our hands are already full of selfish pursuits and priorities. Surely, we were not hoping to receive such a precious gift as divine love without picking up the cross, were we?"[115]

Daily dying to self must be the chosen lifestyle of every faithful Christian (Romans 6:6; Galatians 2:20; 5:24; 6:14). It means setting our mind on God's interests, not our own. It means denying ourselves of sinful pleasures (Colossians 3:5-10; Titus 2:11-12), but it also means dying to our natural instinct for self-preservation when faced with opposition. This connects with Jesus' warning that if we are ashamed of Him, He will be ashamed of us. In other words, if we are ashamed of being identified as His disciple for fear of persecution, and we deny Him to save our own necks, He will deny us (Matthew 10:33; see John 9:18-23; 12:42-43).

The hardest thing in the world to do is to die to self. The old self vigorously resists death. But Jesus has other plans for us. In his book *Born Crucified*, L. E. Maxwell wrote, "What is more logical than a crucified Christ so that he may have crucified followers? . . . . God forbid that we should be 'saved by crucifixion and yet saved from crucifixion.' The disciple is not above his Lord."[116]

The Principle According to the Gospel of Luke

Even later in His ministry Jesus taught the principle again, but this time in the context of being prepared for His return. The verses preceding the principle describe how His coming will catch people by surprise, as did Noah's Flood and the destruction of Sodom. Hendriksen comments:

> In the present context those who are represented as trying to hang on to their life, and losing it, are the earth-bound people of Noah's day and of Lot's day, including definitely also Lot's wife, and all those similarly minded. That they are indeed losers will become apparent especially on the day of Christ's return. On that day the preservation and victory of the people who have shown the opposite attitude, that of self-denial and self-sacrifice, out of love for their Savior, will also become publicly manifest.

At Christ's return mankind splits in two, in line with the spiritual division that had occurred earlier.[117]

Immediately before saying, "Whoever seeks to keep his life will lose it, and whoever loses his life will preserve it," Jesus warned, "Remember Lot's wife" (Luke 17:32-33; see Genesis 19:17, 24-26). Apparently, instead of thinking about God's mercy in sparing her and her family from certain destruction, Lot's wife looked back to the city where her home was. What a costly price she paid for turning her head! Are we letting the world turn ours?

On an earlier occasion a man promised Jesus, "I will follow You, Lord; but first permit me to say good-bye to those at home." Although he began well—"I will follow You, Lord . . ."—he then spoiled it by adding "but first . . . ." Jesus replied, "No one, after putting his hand to the plow and looking back, is fit for the kingdom of God" (Luke 9:61-62).

The Principle According to the Gospel of John

The fourth time Jesus taught this principle was during His last week, with the cross looming over Him. Jesus knew full well what horrors lay ahead (John 12:27, 32-33). What if He had loved His life in this world too much to give it up? But as He told Philip and Andrew,

> The hour has come for the Son of Man to be glorified. Truly, truly, I say to you, unless a grain of wheat falls into the earth and dies, it remains alone; but if it dies, it bears much fruit. **He who loves his life loses it, and he who hates his life in this world will keep it to life eternal.** If anyone serves Me, he must follow Me; and where I am, there My servant will be also; if anyone serves Me, the Father will honor him (John 12:23-26, emphasis added).

In the words of Janice Greenleaf, "In the metaphor of the wheat seed, He spoke of the necessity of His death to bring life. Then, He said all men must lose their lives to find the eternal life He offered. After all, how can anyone find the new life if he or she will not turn loose of the old one? . . . . It was a radical revelation . . . ."[118]

What did Jesus mean by hating one's life in this world? Often Jesus used vivid language to make a strong point. Earlier He had said with even greater bluntness:

> If anyone comes to Me, and does not hate his own father and mother and wife and children and brothers and sisters, yes, and even his own life, he cannot be My disciple. Whoever does not carry his own cross and come after Me cannot be My disciple (Luke 14:26-27).

Obviously, Jesus was not advocating hatred of family in the usual sense of hate—this would contradict too many other passages in the Bible, as well as Jesus' own teachings. In a marginal note on Luke 14:26 the New American Standard Bible explains that hatred of family and one's own life means "by comparison of his love for Me." In other words, Christ must come first. Our love for Him must far exceed all other affections.

Paul is an example of one who hated his life in this world: ". . . bonds and afflictions await me. But I do not consider my life of any account as dear to myself . . ." (Acts 20:23-24). "For I am ready not only to be bound, but even to die at Jerusalem for the name of the Lord Jesus" (Acts 21:13). "But even if I am being poured out as a drink offering upon the sacrifice and service of your faith, I rejoice and share my joy with you all" (Philippians 2:17). If Paul had loved his life so much that he was unwilling to give it up for Christ, could he be Christ's disciple and would he inherit eternal life? But because Paul "hated" his life in this world, he could look forward to the reward awaiting him. In losing he gained. Expecting to be executed soon, Paul wrote,

> For I am already being poured out as a drink offering, and the time of my departure has come. I have fought the good fight, I have finished the course, I have kept the faith; in the future there is laid up for me the crown of righteousness, which the

Lord, the righteous Judge, will award to me on that day; and not only to me, but also to all who have loved His appearing (2 Timothy 4:6-8).

As he penned these words from death row in a Roman dungeon, Paul was on the verge of experiencing the fulfillment of Jesus' promise, ". . . he who hates his life in this world will keep it to life eternal." He was almost there, and he could hardly wait!

Sadly, not all of his co-workers shared his perspective. Only two verses later, Paul lamented, ". . . Demas, having loved this present world, has deserted me and gone to Thessalonica . . . ." In seeking his own selfish interests, Demas had, like Lot's wife, looked back. But Paul was willing to sacrifice this world for the next. Who made the better bargain—Demas or Paul? We know how Paul felt as his end neared. How do you suppose Demas felt when he was about to leave "this present world"—for what? With Demas at one end of the save/lose—lose/save spectrum and Paul at the other, where do we stand?

The Man Who Did It His Way

Jerusalem was in deep trouble. In view of the Babylonians' impending conquest of the city, Jeremiah offered the citizens of Jerusalem two mutually exclusive options:

> Thus says the LORD, "He who stays in this city will die by the sword and by famine and by pestilence, but he who goes out to the Chaldeans [Babylonians] will live and have his own life as booty and stay alive . . . . This city will certainly be given into the hand of the army of the king of Babylon and he will capture it" (Jeremiah 38:2-3).

To say the least, Jeremiah's message was not well received (Jeremiah 38:4ff.). He was branded a traitor for advocating surrender, and yet that is exactly what God had told him to say.

Jeremiah urged King Zedekiah to cooperate:

> Thus says the LORD God of hosts, the God of Israel, "If you will

indeed go out to the officers of the king of Babylon, then you will live, this city will not be burned with fire, and you and your household will survive. But if you will not go out to the officers of the king of Babylon, then this city will be given over to the hand of the Chaldeans; and they will burn it with fire, and you yourself will not escape from their hand" (Jeremiah 38:17-18).

Faced with this choice, Zedekiah decided to ignore God's warning. He and his men tried escaping the city by night, but just as Jeremiah had warned him, they were captured and the city was destroyed. He could have spared himself and his city untold grief if he had believed God and surrendered. As a result, Zedekiah witnessed the slaughter of his sons, was blinded, and then taken away to Babylon in chains, never to return (Jeremiah 39:1-8; Ezekiel 12:12-13).

If only he had listened! Jeremiah had presented him with a paradox: surrender and live. In his futile attempt to save his life, he became the loser, just as God said he would. His foolish choice made a believer of him, but by then it was too late.

Jesus tells us that if we will lose our life for His sake, we will find it; but if we try to save our life, we will lose it. "Keepers, losers; losers, finders." The stakes are far higher for us than for Zedekiah. We have much more to gain than he did, and far more to lose. Will we learn from his example?

Jesus, too, looked beyond His sacrifice to what the sacrifice would bring: ". . . unless a grain of wheat falls into the earth and dies, it remains alone; but if it dies, it bears much fruit" (John 12:24). ". . . fixing our eyes on Jesus . . . **who for the joy set before Him** endured the cross, despising the shame, and has sat down at the right hand of the throne of God" (Hebrews 12:2, emphasis added).

Are We Willing to Be a Paradox People?

On the computer I use, the type size and font have a default setting for 11-point Calibri. Usually I prefer 12-point Times Roman. But to change it, I have to consciously take the steps to reset it. Likewise, the default setting in life, it seems, is self-interest. "Looking out for number one" comes so naturally we don't even have to think about it. But just as with a computer setting, we have a choice, and if we want to change from self-interest to God's interests, we must consciously and consistently choose it. We can either do what comes naturally and hold on to self, or we can take Jesus at His word and let go of self. Which motto will we choose: "Me First" or "Christ First"? Letting go of self gives new meaning to the phrase, "looking out for Number One." Christ is truly Number One; I'm not. But the delightful irony is that when I let Him be first, life turns out so much better for me in the long run. I have to keep reminding myself of that. Default living isn't really living. Charles Kingsley said, ". . . if you want to be miserable yourself, and a maker of misery to others, the way is easy enough. Only be selfish, and it is done at once . . . . Think about yourself; about what you want, what you like, what respect people ought to pay you, what people think of you . . . ." [119]

But if we will develop the servant mindset instead, we will discover what Alexander Maclaren meant, "To be delivered from making myself my great object, and to be delivered from the undue value set upon having and keeping our possessions, are the twin factors of true blessedness. It is heaven on earth to love and give oneself away." [120]

Principle/Paradox/Promise

Notice where Jesus is in our principle. Not in the warning part ("He who has found his life will lose it . . . ."), but in the promise part (". . . he who has lost his life for My sake will find it."). But note: His promise that we will find true life does not even begin to take effect until after we take the decisive step of dying to self. We cannot enjoy the benefits of Jesus' promise without first trying it out for ourselves. In the familiar words of the old gospel hymn:

But we never can prove
The delights of His love
Until all on the altar we lay;
For the favor He shows,
And the joy He bestows,
Are for those who will trust and obey.[121]

But can Jesus be trusted to keep His promise of eternal life? Isn't His willingness to say *no* to Himself for our sake more than sufficient evidence of His credibility? He has only our best interests at heart. It is precisely because Jesus was willing to live—and die—by the principle He taught us, that we have the same opportunity. But we have a choice: We can die to live, or we can live to die. Referring to these opposite choices, Kerry Williams writes:

> The world says, "Live it up." God says, "Exercise self-control." The world says, "Take your revenge." God says, "Love your enemies." The world says, "Be first." God says, "Put others before yourself." Christian living is almost always exactly the opposite of what the world values.
>
> Look at how God tells us to live for others and not ourselves. Selfishness is so easy. Self-preservation and gratification seem to be hard-wired into our human makeup. In fact, self-centered thinking is powerful and controlling, and we are often blinded to the fact that we are mastered by it. Isn't selfishness really the root of all sin and ugliness?
>
> How do we defeat selfishness when it lurks in every shadow of our souls? We resist it every day! We fight it with kindness and service. When we feel consumed with self-pity, we must turn our emotions outward rather than inward. In other words, we must be intentional to fight it. Jesus said we have to decide to put others first and place ourselves last. When can we start? Right now! How often will we need to renew our commitment to this decision? Every day![122]

When we trust Jesus' promise enough to act on it, we discover that the life we lose really wasn't worth living after all, and that what we gain in the exchange is worth far more than anything we had been holding onto for dear life. Frederick Buechner said it well:

> Inspection stickers used to have printed on the back "Drive carefully—the life you save may be your own." That is the wisdom of men in a nutshell.
>
> What God says, on the other hand, is "The life you save is the life you lose." In other words, the life you clutch, hoard, guard, and play safe with is in the end a life worth little to anybody, including yourself, and only a life given away for love's sake is a life worth living. To bring his point home, God shows us a man who gave his life away to the extent of dying a national disgrace without a penny in the bank . . . . In terms of men's wisdom, he was a Perfect Fool, and anybody who thinks he can follow him without making something like the same kind of fool of himself is laboring under not a cross but a delusion.[123]

Questions:

1. Why was Jesus fond of using paradox to make a point?

2. How does the losing-to-gain principle work in athletic training, getting an education, marriage, and retirement planning?

3. For the Christian, in what sense could it be possible to "have the best of both worlds"?

4. What can we learn from the "but first" statements in Luke 9:59-62.

5. What is there about letting go of self that can be such a challenge?

6. What could make it easier for us to say *no* to self and *yes* to Christ?

CHAPTER 9

How to Be Exalted

**Whoever exalts himself shall be humbled;
and whoever humbles himself shall be exalted.**

(Matthew 23:12)

S everal years ago I was asked to lead a prayer at a civic breakfast. Arriving in plenty of time, I went through the buffet, then looked for a seat near the front where I would not have far to walk to the microphone. As I was preparing to take my seat, someone came up and informed me that my table of choice was reserved. It had no reserved sign on it, so how was I to know? But meekly, I chose another table. Since then, I have used my gaffe to illustrate Jesus' teaching:

> When you are invited by someone to a wedding feast, do not take the place of honor, for someone more distinguished than you may have been invited by him, and he who invited you both will come and say to you, "Give your place to this man," and then in disgrace you proceed to occupy the last place. But when you are invited, go and recline at the last place, so that when the one who has invited you comes, he may say to you, "Friend, move up higher"; then you will have honor in the sight of all who are at the table with you. **For everyone who exalts himself will be humbled, and he who humbles himself will be exalted** (Luke 14:8-11, emphasis added).

On two other occasions Jesus taught this principle, aiming it at the Pharisees who sought glory from others (Matthew 23:5-12). And then in Luke 18:9-14 Jesus exposes pride in all its ugliness:

> And He also told this parable to some people who trusted in themselves that they were righteous, and viewed others with contempt: "Two men went up into the temple to pray, one a Pharisee and the other a tax collector. The Pharisee stood and was praying this to himself: 'God, I thank You that I am not like

other people: swindlers, unjust, adulterers, or even like this tax collector. I fast twice a week; I pay tithes of all that I get.' But the tax collector, standing some distance away, was even unwilling to lift up his eyes to heaven, but was beating his breast, saying, 'God, be merciful to me, the sinner!' I tell you, this man went to his house justified rather than the other; for everyone who exalts himself will be humbled, but he who humbles himself will be exalted" (emphasis added).

According to Jimmy Allen, "One Sunday morning a group of Christians studied that parable in a Bible class. Following the lesson, the brother who led the closing prayer said, 'Father, we are thankful we are not like that Pharisee.'"[124]

It isn't hard to find someone to measure ourselves by and make ourselves look pretty good by comparison. But when we contrast ourselves with the absolute goodness of God and the purity of Christ, who can boast? As George A. Buttrick put it, "A mountain shames a molehill until both are humbled by the stars."[125]

God Opposes the Proud

Jesus' principle, "Whoever exalts himself shall be humbled," is reflected in the Old Testament:

> Everyone who is proud in heart is an abomination to the LORD;
> Assuredly, he will not be unpunished (Proverbs 16:5).

> Do not claim honor in the presence of the king,
> And do not stand in the place of great men;
> For it is better that it be said to you, "Come up here,"
> Than for you to be placed lower in the presence of the prince,
> Whom your eyes have seen (Proverbs 25:6-7).

> The proud look of man will be abased
> And the loftiness of man will be humbled,
> And the LORD alone will be exalted in that day.
> For the LORD of hosts will have a day of reckoning
> Against everyone who is proud and lofty
> And against everyone who is lifted up,
> That he may be abased.

. . . .

The pride of man will be humbled
And the loftiness of men will be abased;
And the LORD alone will be exalted in that day . . .
(Isaiah 2:11-12, 17).

God hates pride (Psalm 18:27; 101:5; Proverbs 6:16-19)! Just as tall objects attract lightning, so pride calls down the wrath of God. If you are out in an open field and lightning is an immediate threat, the recommended posture is crouching down with head lowered. In other words, *make yourself as small a target as possible.*

The following examples show us not only what God thinks of pride but also what He does to those who are too full of themselves.

Example #1: The High Cost of Pride

Uzziah was king of Judah. Greatly helped by God, Uzziah let his successes go to his head. He forgot the Source of his accomplishments. He became so proud that he marched into the temple one day to offer incense. Not being a priest, he was unqualified to serve in the temple; therefore the priests ordered him out. Their opposition angered him, and at that very moment God struck him with leprosy. He was compelled to vacate his palace and turn the kingship over to his son Jotham (2 Chronicles 26:4-5, 7-8, 15-21). Because Uzziah exalted himself, God humbled him. Every day of his life from that day onward, he was reminded that pride doesn't pay. Uzziah died a leper. "Uzziah the king, Uzziah the leper, Uzziah the corpse."[126]

Example #2: A Braggart's Empty Boast

Sennacherib, king of Assyria, sent his officials to intimidate the people of Jerusalem. He boasted, "Who among all the gods of the lands have delivered their land from my hand, that the LORD should deliver Jerusalem from my hand?" (2 Kings 18:35). God countered:

Whom have you reproached and blasphemed?
And against whom have you raised your voice,
And haughtily lifted up your eyes?
Against the Holy One of Israel!

....

Because of your raging against Me,
And because your arrogance has come up to My ears,
Therefore I will put My hook in your nose,
And my bridle in your lips,
And I will turn you back by the way which you came
(2 Kings 19:22, 28; see Isaiah 10:5-19).

God made good on His threat. During the night an angel struck dead the entire camp of 185,000 Assyrian soldiers outside Jerusalem—and that without the people of Jerusalem having to strike a single blow. God did it all. His army wiped out, Sennacherib withdrew to his capital city Nineveh and was later assassinated by his own sons. This incident is so significant that God preserved it in three books of the Old Testament (2 Kings 18-19; 2 Chronicles 32; Isaiah 36-37). In the British Museum is a prism on which is inscribed Sennacherib's own account of his campaign against Jerusalem. He wrote, ". . . Hezekiah himself I shut up in Jerusalem, his capital city, like a bird in a cage . . . ."[127]

True to a point, but he didn't tell the rest of the story. No wonder.

Example #3: "The bigger they come, the harder they fall."

King Nebuchadnezzar of Babylon was the most powerful man of his day. He asked Daniel the prophet to interpret his troubling dream about a lofty tree that was cut down. Daniel explained that this meant the king would be greatly humbled until he acknowledged God's supremacy.

Twelve months later he was walking on the roof of the royal palace of Babylon. The king reflected and said, "Is this not

Babylon the great, which I myself have built as a royal residence by the might of my power and for the glory of my majesty?" (Daniel 4:29-30).

It was then that Nebuchadnezzar's nightmare came true. Years later, Daniel explained to King Belshazzar what had happened:

O king, the Most High God granted sovereignty, grandeur, glory and majesty to Nebuchadnezzar your father. Because of the grandeur which He bestowed on him, all the peoples, nations and men of every language feared and trembled before him . . . . But when his heart was lifted up and his spirit became so proud that he behaved arrogantly, he was deposed from his royal throne and his glory was taken away from him. He was also driven away from mankind, and his heart was made like that of beasts, and his dwelling place was with the wild donkeys. He was given grass to eat like cattle, and his body was drenched with the dew of heaven until he recognized that the Most High God is ruler over the realm of mankind and that He sets over it whomever He wishes (Daniel 5:18-21).

Nebuchadnezzar learned the hard way, as he finally acknowledged, that God "is able to humble those who walk in pride" (Daniel 4:37). What Mary of Nazareth said of God centuries later certainly applies: "He has scattered those who were proud in the thoughts of their heart. He has brought down rulers from their thrones, and has exalted those who were humble" (Luke 1:51b-52).

Why God Hates Pride

For though the LORD is exalted,
Yet He regards the lowly,
But the haughty He knows from afar (Psalm 138:6).

Why is God so alienated by pride? What is there about arrogance that God finds so detestable?

First, the proud person has a wrong attitude toward God. He does not willingly acknowledge God as his Creator, benefactor, or superior. He does not easily express thanks or offer worship to the One who supremely deserves praise. Repentance is all but impossible for the proud person, who hates to admit that God is right and he has been wrong. Pride and obedience go separate ways, because to obey is to submit one's will to another, and that takes humility. We must acknowledge what pride really is, as the following makes so brutally clear:

> It is my pride that makes me independent of God. It's appealing to me to feel that I am the master of my fate, that I run my own life, call my own shots, go it alone. But that feeling is basic dishonesty. I can't go it alone. I have to get help from other people, and I can't ultimately rely on myself. I'm dependent on God for my next breath. It is dishonest of me to pretend that I'm anything but a man—small, weak, and limited. So, living independent of God is self-delusion. It is not just a matter of pride being an unfortunate little trait and humility being an attractive little virtue; it's my inner psychological integrity that's at stake. When I am conceited, I am lying to myself about what I am. I am pretending to be God, and not man. My pride is the idolatrous worship of myself. And that is the national religion of Hell! [128]

Second, the proud person has a wrong attitude toward others. If he perceives that he lacks what someone else has, he feels envy. Conversely, he is arrogant toward those he considers beneath him (Luke 18:9-12). "Big I, little you."

Third, the proud person has a wrong attitude toward himself (Romans 12:3). His inflated self-evaluation is skewed because he fails to take God and others into account. Keeping God always in view helps us recognize our smallness and dependence on Him for all things. Taking others into account, we realize that God is no respecter of persons.

Addressing the self-satisfied Christians of Laodicea, Jesus said, ". . . you say, 'I am rich, and have become wealthy, and have need of nothing,' and you do not know that you are wretched and miserable and poor and blind and naked" (Revelation 3:17). Their self-assessment was the exact opposite of Christ's evaluation of them. Pride is blind. As Jimmy Allen puts it, "Pride, reduced to its simplest form, is self-centeredness."[129] But in contrast, "The smaller we are the more room God has."[130]

God Exalts the Humble

Jesus' repeated emphasis on humility is later reflected by Peter:

> You younger men, likewise, be subject to your elders; and all of you, clothe yourselves with humility toward one another, for God is opposed to the proud, but gives grace to the humble. Therefore humble yourselves under the mighty hand of God, that He may exalt you at the proper time . . . (1 Peter 5:5-6; see James 4:6-7, 10).

Case Studies in Humility

Having seen examples of those whose pride led to their downfall, we can now see how the positive side of the principle works, as God exalts those who humble themselves.

Example #1: A Sense of Undeserving

Following his victory over Goliath, David could have easily gotten the big head when he heard his praises sung, "Saul has slain his thousands, and David his ten thousands" (1 Samuel 18:7). But instead he remained humble. King Saul had promised his daughter in marriage to anyone who could defeat Goliath. And yet David's response was, "Who am I, and what is my life or my father's family in Israel, that I should be the king's son-in-law" (1 Samuel 18:18; see verse 23). "Who am I?" he asked.

After David became king, he was assured by God, "Your house and your kingdom shall endure before Me forever; your throne shall be established forever." In response, David prayed, "Who am I, O Lord GOD, and what is my house, that You have brought me this far?" (2 Samuel 7:16, 18). Again, "Who am I?"

His life about to come to a close, David led his people in

contributing generously for the construction of the temple to be built by his son, Solomon. "But who am I and who are my people that we should be able to offer as generously as this? For all things come from You, and from Your hand we have given You" (1 Chronicles 29:14).

"Who am I?" David asked this as a young man, in his middle years, and toward the end of his life. It was not false modesty. He sincerely felt he did not deserve the privileges God had granted him.

Think what David could have put on his résumé! In his early days this is how someone evaluated him: "a skillful musician, a mighty man of valor, a warrior, one prudent in speech, and a handsome man; and the LORD is with him" (1 Samuel 16:18). Giant-killer, highly praised by his people, attendant to his king, best friend of Prince Jonathan, chosen by God over his older brothers to become the next ruler of His people Israel. How many could attain such heights without letting pride destroy them? "Who am I?" David asked. Good question. And who, might we ask, are we?

A major ingredient of gratitude and of humility is a sense of how undeserving we are of God's good gifts. In contrast, the person who feels entitled has a hard time being genuinely grateful. Instead, he is more likely to complain that he hasn't been given all that's due him.

We Americans often demand our rights. How blessed we are to have these privileges as citizens! Did we produce them? Did we earn them? Do we deserve them? Does God owe us a thing?

Can't we all say as David did, "Who am I, O Lord God . . . that You have brought Me this far?"

Example #2: A Proud Man Who Learned to Humble Himself

Naaman, the Aramean army commander, enjoyed his king's favor, and yet he was a leper. Desperate for a cure, he followed up on a suggestion made by his wife's young Israelite maidservant, who said the prophet Elisha could help him.

When Naaman arrived at Elisha's door, he was taken aback that the prophet sent his servant instead of coming out personally to meet him. Not only that, but Elisha sent word to dip seven times in the Jordan River if he wished to be cleansed of his leprosy. Incensed by this unexpected turn of events, Naaman abruptly turned to leave, protesting that the rivers back home were better than the Jordan. But his servants reasoned with him, "My father, had the prophet told you to do some great thing, would you not have done it? How much more then, when he says to you, 'Wash, and be clean'?" (2 Kings 5:13). To Naaman's credit, he listened; and when he humbled himself and did exactly what Elisha said, he was cleansed. But not until. His pride had almost gotten the best of him! But when he humbled himself, he found cleansing.

What a contrast between Uzziah, who exalted himself and was struck with leprosy, and Naaman, who humbled himself and was cleansed of leprosy!

Example #3: The Supreme Example of Humility

Jesus practiced what He preached. He had repeatedly taught His disciples that they must humble themselves in service to others. They were slow to learn. Finally, at the Last Supper He drove the point home by washing the disciples' feet (John 13). Everett F. Harrison comments, "Here we learn what true humility is—not the miserable habit of thinking mean thoughts about oneself, but engaging in self-giving that brings good to others."[131]

Not only did He repeatedly teach the need for humbling oneself, but no one exemplified this better than He, as illustrated so well in what William Barclay calls "the greatest and the most moving passage that Paul ever wrote about Jesus."[132]

> Have this attitude in yourselves which was also in Christ Jesus, who, although He existed in the form of God, did not regard

equality with God a thing to be grasped, but emptied Himself, taking the form of a bond-servant, and being made in the likeness of men. Being found in appearance as a man, he humbled Himself by becoming obedient to the point of death, even death on a cross. For this reason also, God highly exalted Him, and bestowed on Him the name which is above every name, so that at the name of Jesus every knee will bow, of those who are in heaven and on earth and under the earth, and that every tongue will confess that Jesus Christ is Lord, to the glory of God the Father (Philippians 2:5-11).

Philippians 2:5-11

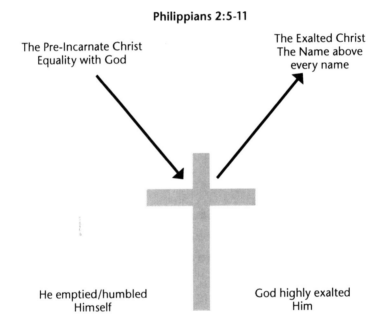

The Pre-Incarnate Christ
Equality with God

The Exalted Christ
The Name above
every name

He emptied/humbled
Himself

God highly exalted
Him

The verses preceding this great passage indicate why Paul felt it necessary to emphasize the One who demoted Himself more than anyone ever had or ever would:

Do nothing from selfishness or empty conceit, but with humility of mind regard one another as more important than yourselves; do not merely look out for your own personal interests, but also for the interests of others (Philippians 2:3-4).

Then Paul drives this point home by holding up Christ as the perfect model of selfless humility that should characterize His followers. In His death He could not have humbled Himself any more than He did. A. T. Robinson calls the cross "The bottom rung in the ladder from the Throne of God."[133]

In the same chapter Paul cites three more examples demonstrating this principle. First, Paul told the Philippians that he himself was willing to be "poured out as a drink offering upon the sacrifice and service of your faith" (Philippians 2:17). Second, Paul was planning to send Timothy, "For I have no one else of kindred spirit who will genuinely be concerned for your welfare. For they all seek after their own interests, not those of Christ Jesus" (Philippians 2:20- 21). And third, Epaphroditus had become deathly ill in delivering a gift to Paul from the Philippians. Paul urged them to "hold men like him in high regard; because he came close to death for the work of Christ, risking his life to complete what was deficient in your service to me" (Philippians 2:29-30). Paul, Timothy, and Epaphroditus—all were examples of that Christ-like spirit of humility that puts others ahead of self.

What Helps Us Humble Ourselves?

"How to" books are popular, but do you think that a book titled *How to Humble Yourself* could become a best-seller? Is humbling ourselves just too bitter a pill to swallow?

D. L. Moody was right in saying, "There is no harder lesson to learn than the lesson of humility."[134] How humiliating it is to acknowledge our complete inadequacy apart from Christ, but how it frees us to admit it! What then can help make this bitter pill somewhat easier to swallow? How do we humble ourselves?

First, we acknowledge God as the Source of all our strengths. Paul found it necessary to correct the divided Corinthian church:

> . . . that no one of you will become arrogant in behalf of one against the other. For who regards you as superior? What do

you have that you did not receive? And if you did receive it, why do you boast as it you had not received it? (1 Corinthians 4:6-7; see 1 Peter 4:10).

Second, we need an increased awareness of how superior God is to us. When God confronted Job with question after question he could not answer, Job's response was:

Behold, I am insignificant; what can I reply to You?
I lay my hand on my mouth (Job 40:4).

I know that You can do all things,
And that no purpose of Yours can be thwarted.
. . . .
Therefore I have declared that which I did not understand,
Things too wonderful for me, which I did not know.
. . . .
I have heard of You by the hearing of the ear;
But now my eye sees You;
Therefore I retract,
And I repent in dust and ashes (Job 42:2, 3, 5-6;
see Isaiah 6:1-5; Luke 5:8).

Third, we need a greater consciousness of our own sin. Paul is a good example of one who was willing to admit that he had fallen short of the glory of God (1 Corinthians 15:9; 1 Timothy 1:12-17). The Prodigal Son could not begin his recovery until he was willing to confess, "Father, I have sinned against heaven and in your sight; I am no longer worthy to be called your son" (Luke 15:21).

Fourth, we must strongly desire a restored relationship with God.

He has told you, O man, what is good;
And what does the LORD require of you
But to do justice, to love kindness,
And to walk humbly with your God? (Micah 6:8).

But to this one I will look,
To him who is humble and contrite of spirit, and who trembles at
My word (Isaiah 66:2).

For thus says the high and exalted One
Who lives forever, whose name is Holy,
"I dwell on a high and holy place,
And also with the contrite and lowly of spirit
In order to revive the spirit of the lowly
And to revive the heart of the contrite" (Isaiah 57:15).

God feels welcome in the humble heart. Citing the three passages above, Larry Deason writes, "God's revelation that 'the way up is down' did not suddenly begin with the New Testament teaching. The prophets had spoken clearly."[135]

Fifth, we realize that we can avoid the penalties of pride when we humble ourselves.

Pride goes before destruction,
And a haughty spirit before stumbling (Proverbs 16:18).

In other words, "If we do not learn humility, we will learn humiliation."[136]

Sixth, Jesus promises to exalt us when we humble ourselves. There is nothing wrong with aiming for exaltation—if we do it God's way. When James and John requested the places of highest honor on either side of Jesus in His kingdom, He explained:

You know that the rulers of the Gentiles lord it over them, and their great men exercise authority over them. It is not this way among you, but whoever wishes to become great among you shall be your servant, and whoever wishes to be first among you shall be your slave; just as the Son of Man did not come to be served, but to serve, and to give His life a ransom for many (Matthew 20:25-28).

Jesus' values so often run counter to the norm, the expected, the conventional. To go up you must go down. To live you must die. To win you must surrender. To gain you must lose. Jesus' values go against the tide of popular opinion, against the grain of our pride, against the bent of our natural inclinations. It reminds me of a lock on the front door of our church building. When you insert the key to open it, you must turn it the opposite way from most door locks. It feels odd, but it works. So with Jesus. Obeying Him goes contrary to our instincts. It takes some getting used to, to say the least, and yet doing it His way opens the door to His greatest blessings.

Regarding humility, the message of Jesus to us is essentially this:

> If you really want to go up,
> You must first be willing
> to go down. I did.
> So can you.
> Follow
> Me.

Questions:

1. Study the following examples of pride brought low: Babel (Genesis 11:1-9), Edom (Jeremiah 49:16), and Herod Agrippa (Acts 12:20-23).

2. What factors tend to contribute to pride? (Deuteronomy 8:11-18; Esther 3:1-2, 5; Romans 2:17-20; 12:16; 1 Corinthians 8:1; 1 Timothy 6:17)

3. In what specific ways did Jesus demonstrate humility during His time on earth?

4. What did Jesus mean when He said, "Whoever then humbles himself as this child, he is the greatest in the kingdom of heaven" (Matthew 18:4)?

5. Study the following passages on pride and humility: Proverbs 18:12; 29:23; Romans 12:3; James 4:13-17. Discuss what you learn from these.

6. What does Jesus teach about humility in John 13:1-17? In what practical ways can it be applied today?

CHAPTER 10

Strength Through Weakness

*"My grace is sufficient for you,
for power is perfected in weakness."*

(2 Corinthians 12:9)

M any years ago, feeling tense and overworked, I took a short course in stress management. We were handed a questionnaire to which we were to respond by checking the box for "Agree" or "Disagree." At the end of the questionnaire, our responses were tallied and evaluated. Regarding one of the sets of questions, it says, "The higher the total, the greater your agreement with the irrational idea that you need something other or stronger or greater than yourself to rely on." I scored 6 out of 10. The reason for such a low score is that I had agreed with such statements as these: "Everyone needs someone he can depend on for help and advice" and "People need a source of strength outside themselves."[137] According to the presuppositions of those who created this test, my answers were irrational. But I'm convinced that this questionnaire says more about the test-makers than it does about the test-takers.

Wouldn't it be interesting to know how the apostle Paul would score? Did he believe he needed help from above? If so, was he irrational? Of all the people mentioned in the New Testament, aside from Christ, Paul is the one we know the most about. Our two main sources of information on Paul are the book of Acts and his letters to churches and individuals. Of all his letters, according to D. Edmond Hiebert, "Second Corinthians is the most autobiographical . . . . In it he bares his heart and life as in none of his other writings."[138] One particularly insightful passage in this letter indicates how he would have answered the questions cited above. Here he describes how his attitude had been totally transformed:

Because of the surpassing greatness of the revelations, for this reason, to keep me from exalting myself, there was given me a thorn in the flesh, a messenger of Satan to torment me—to keep me from exalting myself! Concerning this I implored the Lord three times that it might leave me. And He has said to me, "My grace is sufficient for you, for power is perfected in weakness." Most gladly, therefore, I will rather boast about my weaknesses, so that the power of Christ may dwell in me. Therefore I am well content with weaknesses, with insults, with distresses, with persecutions, with difficulties, for Christ's sake; for when I am weak, then I am strong (2 Corinthians 12:7-10).

Why the Thorn?

For centuries, Bible students have speculated on what Paul's thorn was. Was it poor eyesight? Epilepsy? Malaria? Whatever the thorn was, Paul found it troublesome enough to beg the Lord three times to remove it. But still the thorn remained. Why did the Lord not grant his request? Was it that Paul didn't have enough faith? Was God using the thorn to punish Paul for his sins? Or did God simply not care enough to do anything about it? None of the above. Why then was Paul's petition denied? The Lord did not remove the thorn because it was not His will to remove it. But evidently the thorn made Paul physically weak. In view of the great task He had given Paul, why would the Lord want Paul to be weak?

God, Satan, and the Thorn

What did Paul mean when he said that the thorn was "a messenger of Satan to torment me"? Hurndall may be right when he says of the thorn:

It was used of Satan to annoy, pain, depress, and harass Paul, and with the hope that it would hinder his great work. Satanic malice rejoiced in the anticipation that it might prove the last straw upon the camel's back. Paul interfered much with the devil's kingdom; it is no wonder that the devil sought to interfere with him. Satan can afford to leave some people alone; but if we faithfully attack his kingdom and his rule, we may expect reprisals.[139]

What's interesting is that both God and Satan had something to do with Paul's thorn. Apparently, what was going on here was similar to what Job experienced. Satan requested God's permission to afflict Job, asserting that taking his blessings away would cause Job to curse God. But God had confidence in Job's integrity, and His confidence was not misplaced. In Paul's case, the irony is that apparently Satan intended for the thorn to defeat Paul, while God was using the thorn to strengthen him. But instead of defeating either Job or Paul, Satan was himself defeated.

A New Perspective

The turning point in Paul's attitude came when the Lord revealed His reasons: "My grace is sufficient for you." In other words, "My grace is enough for you—it is all you need. I will help you get through this."

And yet, even though the thorn remained, something did change. The change was not in the Lord, nor in the thorn, but in Paul. Once he came to see the thorn's purpose, not only did he stop praying for its removal, but he actually welcomed it as the blessing God meant for it to be. In all this Paul grew. A worthwhile study can be made of the spiritual growth Paul experienced after becoming a disciple of Christ. The same chapter that records his conversion also says that he "kept increasing in strength" (Acts 9:22). But Paul was quick to credit the Lord as the Source of his strength (Philippians 4:13; Colossians 1:29; 1 Timothy 1:12; 2 Timothy 4:17). As a result of having the thorn, Paul came to realize, "Most gladly, therefore, I will rather boast about my weaknesses, so that the power of Christ may dwell in me."

King Uzziah, mentioned briefly in the last chapter, enjoyed heady successes in battle, construction projects, and agricultural pursuits. ". . . as long as he sought the LORD, God prospered him

. . . . he was marvelously helped until he was strong. But when he became strong, his heart was so proud that he acted corruptly, and he was unfaithful to the Lord his God . . ." (2 Chronicles 26:5, 15-16). God was then compelled to humble Uzziah by making him a lifelong leper. He learned the hard way: "When I am strong, then I am weak."

Paul came to realize that he was better off with his thorn than without it. Without the thorn he was vulnerable to pride because of "the surpassing greatness of the revelations" God was giving him. Evidently Paul received more of these heavenly communications than most if not all of his fellow believers. Alexander Maclaren's observation is well-taken: "Ministers of the Gospel especially should banish all thoughts of their own cleverness, intellectual ability, culture, sufficiency for their work, and learn that only when they are emptied can they be filled, and only when they know themselves to be nothing are they ready for God to work through them."[140]

Humility comes neither easily nor cheaply, and in Paul's case the last thing he needed was a "thornectomy." What he truly needed was not to have the thorn removed but to have his thinking renewed (Romans 12:2; Ephesians 4:23). What he needed was a major attitude adjustment, and that's exactly what he did receive. In all this, the thorn provided Paul with at least two tremendous blessings: 1) he was saved from pride, and 2) he experienced great spiritual growth as he learned to view the thorn from God's perspective. In addition to what Paul himself gained, we are encouraged by reading about his struggle and ultimate victory. What God did in Paul's life He can do in ours.

From this agonizing experience, Paul discovered a dynamic principle at work in his life. Paradoxically, when he was weak (as a result of hardships), he found himself growing stronger as he learned to draw on the Lord's power. Not everyone understands this, as Charles B. Hodge Jr. observes:

Our culture is far more concerned about feeling good than being good. Sin brings damnation from God. No one is condemned for hurting. All are condemned for sin. Sin makes one evil; hurting does not! Yet we strive to live pain-free lives. We should strive to live sin-free lives. We fear suffering more than sin! [141]

The Role of Suffering

The complex issue of why we suffer is beyond the scope of this book. The Bible teaches us that not all suffering has the same cause. For example, God warned that He would punish Israel if they did not obey His command to expel the Canaanites: ". . . those whom you let remain of them will become as pricks in your eyes and as thorns in your sides . . ." (Numbers 33:55). But Paul's thorn in the flesh was not to punish him for his sin but to keep him from sinning.

No right-thinking person enjoys suffering—Paul certainly didn't—but if we really are thinking right, we will learn as Paul did to see the good that can come from our suffering (Romans 5:3-5; 8:28; Philippians 1:12-14; see Hebrews 12:4-11; James 1:2-4; 1 Peter 1:6-7). At first he chafed under the thorn—how it hurt! Later he could say, ". . . I am well content with weaknesses, with insults, with distresses, with persecutions, with difficulties, for Christ's sake; for when I am weak, then I am strong." J. I. Packer writes, "The weaker we feel, the harder we lean. And the harder we lean, the stronger we grow spiritually . . . ." [142]

Instead of continuing to pray, "I don't want this thorn," Paul learned to say, "I need this thorn." Yes, it still hurt, but it didn't harm. Not only did it do him no harm, but he came to see it as a hurt that helped. As Philip Yancey says,

Indeed, in an odd sort of way, human beings need problems more than we need solutions. Problems stretch us and press us toward dependence on God. As the Bible reiterates, success represents a far greater danger. Samson, Saul, Solomon, and scores of others show that success leads toward pride and self-satisfaction, a path away from dependence and often a prelude to a fall. [143]

How Paul Came to Terms with His Thorn

What enabled Paul to move from being so aggravated by his thorn to accepting it as a blessing in disguise? His change of perspective came when the Lord told him: "My grace is sufficient for you, for power is perfected in weakness." In other words, "I will give you the grace to endure it, and your very weakness is My opportunity to demonstrate My power at work in your life."

Paul came to realize that the thorn was an antidote to pride. Twice Paul says that the thorn was given to him "to keep me from exalting myself." Better to hurt and keep humble than to feel good and go bad. "If Paul had been healthy, he might have congratulated himself on his own efforts. When he saw the results of his work, he knew that it must have been God's work." [144]

God's answer gave Paul the divine perspective he lacked when agonizing over the thorn. Once the Lord explained it, Paul experienced one of those "Aha!" moments: "Oh, now I see!" How different the thorn looked in this new light! And not only did Paul learn to view his thorn from this new vantage point, but he could now see how any hardship—not just the thorn—could work for his ultimate good.

Learning to Submit

When the Lord denied his plea to have his thorn taken away, what if Paul had reacted by pouting like Jonah, blaming God for not handling the situation the way he thought He should? For Paul to be willing to say, ". . . for when I am weak, then I am strong," and mean it, he had to learn to see suffering through God's eyes, and he had to value his spiritual welfare over his own personal comfort.

As it was, Paul not only came to see the benefits of the thorn but realized that the Lord's *no* was an ultimate *yes*. As Hillyer says, "The Lord's 'No' was a rich positive which empowered the rest of Paul's ministry." [145] Every day that Paul lived with his thorn was another day he was sustained by God's grace—grace sufficient not only to endure the thorn but also to embrace it as a blessing.

Before his new perspective, Paul had two problems: 1) the thorn itself, and 2) his aggravation because of the thorn. After his thinking was enlightened by the Lord's explanation, Paul still had the thorn but no longer was he upset about it. And not only was he free of frustration, but there was a sense of joy in its place. Now instead of fretting about the thorn, he could use words like *most gladly* and *well content* (vv. 9-10).

In accepting the thorn gracefully, Paul demonstrated at least four qualities: 1) a teachable spirit, 2) humble submission to the Lord's will in this matter, 3) a willingness to suffer, and 4) complete trust in the God who knows best. The first chapter of 2 Corinthians shows how Paul grew in this trust:

> For we do not want you to be unaware, brethren, of our affliction which came to us in Asia, that we were burdened excessively, beyond our strength, so that we despaired even of life; indeed, we had the sentence of death within ourselves **so that we would not trust in ourselves, but in God** who raises the dead; who delivered us from so great a peril of death, and will deliver us, He on whom we have set our hope. And He will yet deliver us . . . (2 Corinthians 1:8-10, emphasis added).

As far as we know, Paul had his thorn till the day he died. Tradition says that Paul was beheaded in Rome. When the executioner's axe severed Paul's head from his body, it also separated Paul from his thorn. Since it was a thorn in the flesh, the moment he died he left his flesh, with its embedded thorn, behind. Paul doesn't have his thorn anymore!

Learning to Trust

Is it possible that whenever we feel overwhelmed by our pain, we too could profit from the divine perspective on suffering that helped Paul so much? To gain this insight we must want the same thing God wants—our ultimate good, rather than immediate relief. "All discipline for the moment seems not to be joyful, but sorrowful; yet to those who have been trained by it, **afterwards it yields the peaceful fruit of righteousness**" (Hebrews 12:11, emphasis added). Only by taking this long view of suffering can we benefit the most. As Philip Yancey says, "God seems to value character more than our comfort, often using the very elements that cause us most discomfort as his tools in fashioning that character."[146]

Leaning on What?

By using the thorn, God was trying to teach Paul to lean on Him instead of relying on himself. Isn't this one of the hardest lessons we humans have to learn? The Bible is filled with encouragements to trust God for our help. Here are just a few:

> Those who trust in the LORD
> Are as Mount Zion, which cannot be moved but abides forever (Psalm 125:1).

> Trust in the LORD with all your heart
> And do not lean on your own understanding.
> In all your ways acknowledge Him,
> And He will make your paths straight (Proverbs 3:5-6).

> Behold, God is my salvation,
> I will trust and not be afraid;
> For the LORD GOD is my strength and song,
> And He has become my salvation (Isaiah 12:2).

> The steadfast of mind You will keep in perfect peace,
> Because he trusts in You.
> Trust in the LORD forever,
> For in GOD the LORD, we have an everlasting Rock (Isaiah 26:3-4).

On one occasion God ordered Gideon to lead Israel against the Midianites, even though he was outnumbered by more than four to one. In spite of those odds, God whittled down Gideon's army from 32,000 to 300. That meant that Gideon would be facing 135,000 Midianites with only 300 men—a ratio of 450:1! As a result of God's order to shrink his army, Gideon saw more than 99 percent of his men go home! *What was God thinking?!* Before reducing Gideon's army, God explained, "The people who are with you are too many for Me to give Midian into their hands, for Israel would become boastful, saying, 'My own power has delivered me'" (Judges 7:2). When God then brought victory with only the 300, who could say that Israel should get the credit? Really, did God even need Gideon or his 300? On other occasions, God powerfully demonstrated how easily He could defeat Israel's enemies with no human help at all (2 Kings 7:5-7; 2 Chronicles 20:1-30; 32:1-23). Jonathan would later say to his armor bearer as only the two of them prepared to take on a Philistine garrison, ". . . the LORD is not restrained to save by many or by few" (1 Samuel 14:6). As a result of Jonathan's faith, God blessed him with a great victory. As the people said of Jonathan, ". . . he has worked with God this day" (1 Samuel 14:45).

Not long after, when facing the Philistine giant Goliath (1 Samuel 17), Israel apparently forgot the lesson Gideon learned and Jonathan demonstrated. To them, it was Israel vs. Goliath. When David came on the scene, he viewed the situation entirely differently. To David, it was Goliath vs. God, and he knew which of the two was stronger. When God granted victory to David, He proved powerfully that trust in Him as the Deliverer is richly rewarded.

One difference between Gideon and Paul is that Paul was tempted to rely too much on his own strength, while Gideon felt totally helpless in the face of the enemy. God told Gideon, "Go in this your strength and deliver Israel from the hand of Midian."

"What strength?"—Gideon must have wondered. "O Lord," he protested, "how shall I deliver Israel? Behold, my family is the least in Manasseh, and I am the youngest in my father's house." Gideon was hung up on the personal pronouns "I" and "my." Then God replied, *"Surely I will be with you,* and you shall defeat Midian as one man" (Judges 6:14-16, italics added). It was not Gideon versus Midian, but Gideon's Lord versus the Midianite horde.

Whether we are more like Paul, in danger of becoming prideful, or whether we are like Gideon, lacking in confidence, God is the antidote to both pride and inadequacy. As Paul wrote, "Finally, be strong in the Lord *and in the strength of His might"* (Ephesians 6:10, italics added). This is not self-confidence, but God-confidence. As King Hezekiah said to his people as the city of Jerusalem was being threatened by Sennacherib of Assyria,

> Be strong and courageous, do not fear or be dismayed because of the king of Assyria nor because of all the horde that is with him; for the one with us is greater than the one with him. With him is only an arm of flesh, but with us is the LORD our God to help us and to fight our battles (2 Chronicles 32:7-8).

Hezekiah's ancestor King Jehoshaphat also had his faith tested. Fearing the approach of hostile armies, he gathered his people and led them in prayer: "O our God, will You not judge them? For we are powerless before this great multitude who are coming against us; nor do we know what to do, but our eyes are on You" (2 Chronicles 20:12). God honored Jehoshaphat's faith by giving him a great victory. Commenting on this incident, Robert P. Mullen writes:

> Most people do not like feeling powerless, unable to do what needs to be done. Life does become overwhelming. Our challenge is to fix our eyes on Jesus, the starter and finisher of our faith.
>
> It is all right to know we are powerless, for it is at that point that we can remember to look to God for strength and help.[147]

God's Way and Ours

Mack Lyon recalls,

> Many years ago a man who walked with two aluminum walking aids, whose wife was confined to a wheelchair, came to our congregation seeking support to go into foreign mission work, preaching Christ where Christ had not been preached. Some people objected. They couldn't see the wisdom of sending a man into a foreign country who couldn't even walk and whose wife was nearly an invalid. But he found support and went, and they have spent their lives as very effective missionaries leading people to Christ and establishing congregations there. You see, God's power was magnified in their physical weaknesses. They knew how to lean on God for that wherein they lacked. So must we all. God supplies all our deficiencies when we commit ourselves to Him and to doing His will.[148]

So often God's choices are the direct opposite of ours. His values clash with our values. As Jesus said to the Pharisees, ". . . that which is highly esteemed among men is detestable in the sight of God" (Luke 16:15). What we tend to discount, God can powerfully use to His glory. In all this do you suppose God is trying to teach us something?

> . . . but we preach Christ crucified, to Jews a stumbling block and to Gentiles foolishness, but to those who are the called, both Jews and Greeks, Christ the **power** of God and the wisdom of God. Because the foolishness of God is wiser than men, and the *weakness* of God is stronger than men. For consider your calling, brethren, that there were not many wise according to the flesh, not many mighty, not many noble; but God has chosen the foolish things of the world to shame the wise, and God has chosen the *weak* things of the world to shame the things which are **strong**, and the base things of the world and the despised God has chosen, the things that are not, so that He may nullify the things that are, so that no man may boast before God (1 Corinthians 1:23-29, emphasis added).

And We?

Why did God see fit to preserve this passage on Paul's thorn? Was it not so we too can learn to trust the same God whom Paul served? Even if our suffering is not for the same reason as Paul's, God grace is sufficient for us, too. His power is perfected in our weakness. Like Paul, we can learn to rejoice in our suffering, knowing what it can produce in and for us. In the very next chapter that follows the thorn passage, we read what Paul says of Jesus:

> For indeed He was crucified because of *weakness*, yet He lives because of the **power** of God. For we also are *weak* in Him, yet we will live with Him because of the **power** of God directed toward you (2 Corinthians 13:4, emphasis added).

In the words of Alexander Maclaren,

> . . . when we know ourselves weak, we have taken the first step to strength; just as, when we know ourselves sinners, we have taken the first step to righteousness . . . . All our hollownesses . . . are met with His fullness that fits into them.[149]

Questions:

1. What is there about human nature that does not want to admit the need to depend on God?
2. Why is "self-sufficiency" so dangerous? (Judges 7:3; Proverbs 28:26; Matthew 26:31-35; 1 Corinthians 10:12; Revelation 3:17-18).
3. What advantages are there in learning to depend on God instead of on ourselves?
4. What might Paul have offered God as reasons why he wanted the thorn removed? Would Paul have defended those reasons after he came to understand God's view of it?
5. How does Paul's case illustrate the truth that the way we see things is not always the way God sees them?
6. Can you think of an occasion in your life when you learned to see things God's way, instead of your own?

CHAPTER 11

Faithful in Little Things

**He who is faithful in a very little thing is faithful also in much;
and he who is unrighteous in a very little thing
is unrighteous also in much.**

(Luke 16:10)

Several years ago Sara and I visited Turner Falls in Oklahoma. Twenty-three years before, we viewed Niagara Falls. There is no comparison. There is no question about it; Niagara is much bigger and far more famous. It's possible you've never even heard of Turner.

Even so, we still enjoyed Turner. The water spilled over the cliff in a different way from Niagara. It had its own "personality" and was itself a source of beauty. God made Turner, too.

Once I visited the largest children's museum in the world, in Indianapolis. It had 356,000 square feet with five floors of exhibits. Extremely impressive!

I have also seen a children's museum here in Texas that takes up less space than some houses. (Yes, even Texas does not have a monopoly on the biggest of everything.) Yet I noticed that the children playing there were having a great time. And that was the point.

Big and small. God has placed both in this world. He made the sequoia and the buttercup. He made the mighty Mississippi River and the smallest stream. He made the whale and the lowly earthworm.

Wherever we may be on God's spectrum, we can be what He meant for us to be—and He will be pleased. Jesus was impressed with the generosity of the poor widow, even though others gave much larger amounts (Luke 21:1-4). He knew her heart.

If we cannot sing as well as someone else, let us sing with joy and enthusiasm. If we do not have the health we wish we had, whatever strength we have let us use in His service. If we are not leader material, let's be the best follower we can possibly be. And that's exactly what God would want us to do.

When a Little Matters a Lot

Several years ago while shopping, I found a light blue dress shirt at an amazingly low price. But it had one problem: a small spot. The blemish amounted to far less than one percent of the whole shirt. But it was in a rather obvious place, right above the pocket. If it had been on the shirttail, no problem. And yet, since the shirt was such a bargain, we decided to buy it anyway, hoping that Sara would be able to get the spot out. She tried. Even though she's good at that sort of thing, the smudge wouldn't budge. Now what? It seemed a shame not to be able to wear a sharp-looking, brand-new shirt just because of one little spot. But then Sara came up with a brilliant solution: she stitched a monogram over the spot. Then I could wear it.

Most people would probably hesitate to wear a shirt with an obvious blemish, even if it's a small one. In a sermon on "The Importance of Little Things," Charles Jefferson observes,

> Even the beauty of the dinner table depends on the attention which is given to little things. What spoils a tablecloth? A little spot here and there. What spoils a napkin? A little hole in it. What spoils a plate? A piece chipped out of it. What spoils a knife? A nick in the blade of it.[150]

But in other areas of life which are not so obvious as spots, holes, chips, and nicks, do we sometimes overlook the little things, which may be far more crucial—perhaps even a matter of life or death? How many fatal air crashes have been traced to the failure of one small, inexpensive part that a careless maintenance worker neglected to replace during a routine inspection? James, the Lord's brother, illustrates the power of small things:

> Now if we put the bits into the horses' mouths so that they will

obey us, we direct their entire body as well. Look at the ships also, though they are so great and are driven by strong winds, are still directed by a very small rudder wherever the inclination of the pilot desires. So also the tongue is a small part of the body, and yet it boasts of great things. See how great a forest is set aflame by such a small fire! And the tongue is a fire, the very world of iniquity; the tongue is set among our members as that which defiles the entire body, and sets on fire the course of our life, and is set on fire by hell (James 3:3-6).

Weighing far less than one percent of our total body weight, the tongue exercises an influence far out of proportion to its size. But controlled by Christ, the tongue can have a tremendous impact for good as well.

BIG, **BIGGER, BIGGEST**

In his sermon, "Little Things in a Day of Bigness," Batsell Barrett Baxter began by saying, "History records that men in every age have had a tendency to minimize the value of small things. It is the elephant which gets the attention, not the mouse. From the Tower of Babel to the pyramids, from the Colossus of Rhodes to the modern skyscraper, bigness has captured the attention and the hearts of men." [151]

One of the passages Baxter cited in his lesson was this: "For who has despised the day of small things?" (Zechariah 4:10a). This was said to encourage the Jews who had come back from Babylonian Captivity. They had begun work on rebuilding the temple destroyed by King Nebuchadnezzar many years before. To those who remembered the grand temple of Solomon, this replacement seemed far inferior (Ezra 3:10-12). But God reassured them that in spite of appearances, a glorious future awaited (Haggai 2:3-9).

The Significance of the "Insignificant"
How did Noah build the ark? A board at a time, a nail at a time.

Perhaps when God first told Noah to build a ship the length of one-and-a-half football fields, he may have had that "Where do I begin?" feeling. Wouldn't you?

Yet God gave Noah the strength to make the first cut with his saw and pound that first nail, always keeping his eye on the outcome. "By faith Noah, being warned by God about things not yet seen, in reverence prepared an ark for the salvation of his household . . ." (Hebrews 11:7).

How many nails between the first and the last? How many days before the first deck began to take shape, and the second, and the third? Since his family's safety depended on his work, every single detail took on life-and-death significance, far more so than each component of Apollo 11 and the Eagle landing module from which Neil Armstrong emerged to take the first moonwalk. Not only was the survival of Noah's family at stake, but also all their descendants, including every one of us. Details matter! The painstaking construction of Noah's ark illustrates the little-by-little principle.

Charles Kingsley said, "Let us be content to do little, if God sets us at little tasks. It is but pride and self-will which says, 'Give me something huge to fight,—and I should enjoy that—but why make me sweep the dust?'"[152] (See 2 Kings 5:1-14.) How easy it is to dismiss what appears to be a petty task. But a little may make a lot more difference than we realize:

At 211 degrees, water is hot. At 212 degrees, it boils. And with boiling water, comes steam. And steam can power a locomotive.

One
Degree

Raising the temperature of water by one extra degree means the difference between something that is simply very hot and something that generates enough force to power a machine—a beautiful, uncomplicated metaphor that ideally should feed our every endeavor—consistently pushing us to make the extra effort in every task we undertake. Two hundred and twelve degrees serves as a forceful drill sergeant with its motivating and focused message while adhering to a scientific law—a natural law. It reminds us that **seemingly small things can make tremendous differences.**[153]

What is "Faithful"?

What does it mean to be "faithful in a very little thing," as Jesus said? The Greek word is *pistos*, which is defined as *"faithful, reliable, trustworthy in something."*[154] One day I overheard a couple of college students expressing their anger toward a fellow student who had failed to carry her weight on a group project. They called her a "lame leg." Employers are desperate to find reliable workers. The work ethic of a previous generation has too often been replaced with a "shirk ethic."

Don't you love people you can depend on? So does God. "God is faithful" (1 Corinthians 1:9; 10:13). He keeps all His promises (Joshua 21:45; 23:14-15; 1 Kings 8:56). Christ is faithful (2 Thessalonians 2:3; Hebrews 2:17; 10:23). "If we are faithless, He remains faithful, for He cannot deny Himself" (2 Timothy 2:13). Faithfulness is so ingrained in the character of Christ that it is unthinkable that He could be otherwise. Is it any wonder that He loves to see His faithfulness reflected in His people?

One of the highest compliments paid to anyone in Scripture is to say that the person is faithful. God said of Moses, "He is faithful in all My household" (Numbers 12:7; Hebrews 3:2, 5). The apostle Paul, unquestionably faithful, also appreciated this quality in others. He could speak of "Timothy, who is **my beloved and faithful child** in the Lord" (1 Corinthians 4:17, emphasis added), "Epaphras, our beloved fellow bond-servant, who is a **faithful servant of Christ** on our behalf" (Colossians 1:7), and "Onesimus, **our faithful and beloved brother**" (Colossians 4:9). Could he say the same of us?

Some years ago one of the deacons in our congregation was

presented an award at a chamber of commerce banquet as Employee of the Year. The person who presented his plaque read this tribute to him:

> Joe is available 24 hours a day, seven days a week and never hesitates to arrive at work during any weather condition. He knows that the citizens of Commerce depend on him to take care of their water and wastewater needs and he is always there for them.

Several years later, I read this tribute to the congregation when Joe was appointed as an elder. Since Joe had proved himself a faithful employee and a dependable deacon, we were confident he would be dedicated to the task of shepherding. And he is.

God's work on earth relies on our close attention to the tasks He gives us, down to the smallest detail—faithful in the little things. James Freeman Clarke wrote, "One of the best things in the gospel of Jesus is the stress it lays on small things. It ascribes more value to quality than to quantity; it teaches that God does not ask how much we do, but how we do it." [155]

Just a Shepherd?

David, the future king of Israel, spent his youth taking care of his father Jesse's sheep. One day Jesse sent David with some food for his three oldest brothers in King Saul's army and told him to "look into the welfare of your brothers, and bring back news of them. For Saul and they and all the men of Israel are in the valley of Elah, fighting with the Philistines" (1 Samuel 17:18-19). At least, that's what Jesse *thought* they were doing. In reality they were biding for time. When David arrived, he found the entire Israelite army totally paralyzed by fear of Goliath the Philistine giant. Even King Saul the experienced warrior, who was head and shoulders taller than his countrymen, was afraid of him (1 Samuel 9:2; 10:23; 17:10-11). Twice a day for forty days Goliath had challenged Israel to put forward a warrior to face him.

There were no takers. Not a single Israelite rose to the challenge, including David's three oldest brothers. The Philistines had the Israelites stymied. In view of this shameful situation, David asked,

> What will be done for the man who kills this Philistine and takes away the reproach from Israel? For who is this uncircumcised Philistine, that he should taunt the armies of the living God? (1 Samuel 17:26).

Hearing this, David's oldest brother angrily asked, "Why have you come down? And with whom have you left those few sheep in the wilderness? I know your insolence and the wickedness of your heart; for you have come down in order to see the battle" (1 Samuel 17:28). But God had an entirely different estimation of David:

> He also chose David His servant
> And took him from the sheepfolds;
> From the care of the ewes with suckling lambs He brought him
> To shepherd Jacob His people,
> And Israel His inheritance.
> So he shepherded them according to the integrity of his heart,
> And guided them with his skillful hands (Psalm 78:70-72;
> see 2 Samuel 7:8).

What David's brother disdainfully called "those few sheep" had actually given David the training and experience he needed to learn dependence on God. David credited God for delivering him from the lion and bear that had threatened his flock (1 Samuel 17:34-37). As far as David was concerned, Goliath, for all his height and bluster, was just another lion or bear to take down with God's help. And so down came Goliath, all nine-and-a-half feet of him. Before the day was over, the women of Israel were singing David's praises for slaying the Philistine champion, but how many remember the name of David's brother? Incidentally, God had already rejected his critical older brother Eliab as the one to succeed Saul as king (1 Samuel 16:6-7).

Shepherds of Souls

A family may be a small subset of society, but it is significant far beyond its size. The home is where souls are shaped—for good or bad, for time and eternity. God, who created both the home and the church, uses the smaller unit of the family to determine if a man can handle the far weightier responsibilities of shepherding God's flock, the church. Like David and "those few sheep," a godly husband/father gains invaluable experience as a shepherd of his own family. A qualified elder must be:

> one who manages his own household well, keeping his children under control with all dignity (but if a man does not know how to manage his own household, how will he take care of the church of God?) . . . (1 Timothy 3:4-5; see Titus 1:5-9).

In other words, if he can manage the smaller unit (his family), he can be trusted with the larger sphere (the church). But if he fails on the home front, how could he possibly succeed in leading God's family?

The Character Test

In one of the university Bible classes I taught, a polite young man approached me, graded paper in hand, and said, "I may be shooting myself in the foot, but you gave me credit for a wrong answer." Because I appreciated his honesty and told him so, I did not dock his grade.

Later applying to work with explosives in the military, a position requiring high-security clearance, he asked if I would serve as a reference. I readily agreed. When a federal investigator came to my office regarding his application, I was happy to relate the incident about his quiz grade. If he was truthful about a small matter, couldn't he be trusted to show integrity where national security and people's lives are at stake?

The "Little" Things

What we do with a little reveals our character—who we really are way down deep inside. How we handle the little things is a litmus test of integrity. As Charles Jefferson said,

> If a grocer gives you five cents too much in change, and you do not give it back, then you are dishonest, just as truly dishonest as if you stole a man's watch. If you will steal five cents when you get a chance, the probability is that you will steal a thousand dollars if you ever get a chance.[156]

God charged His people with the crime of robbing Him by shortchanging their giving (Malachi 3:8-10). James Burton Coffman has written, "People who suppose that if they were rich they would give large sums to charity, and yet who give nothing from their meager possessions, are deceiving themselves. What a man does with a little is a fair measure of what he will do with much."[157]

The Lord is looking to see how we handle the pennies, the minutes, and the small details of everyday life. Would God have promoted Joseph to second-in-command in Egypt if he had not already proven himself dependable at three previous stages of his life: as a shepherd of his father's flock, as manager of Potiphar's household, and later as a trusty in prison? If Peter had been a careless manager of his Galilean fishing business, would Jesus have chosen him to become a fisher of men, and would He have entrusted to him the keys of the kingdom of heaven (Matthew 4:18-22; 16:13-19)? Conversely, as treasurer for the apostles, Judas was a petty thief before becoming the world's most infamous traitor (John 12:4-6).

"Faithful with a Few Things"

In one of His parables, Jesus told of a master who entrusted his three servants with various weight measurements of money called talents. By diligent effort, the one entrusted with five talents and the one given two talents each doubled their master's money. When they gave an accounting to their master, he praised each of them, "Well done, good and faithful slave. You were faithful with a few things, I will put you in charge of many things; enter into the joy of your master" (Matthew 25:21). When the third servant lamely admitted that he had done nothing with the one talent entrusted to him, his master censured him as "wicked, lazy .... worthless" (Matthew 25:26, 30). Is it any wonder that he was punished while the other two were promoted? That's only fair.

Life, however, is often unfair. "It's not what you know," they say, "but who you know." Office politics aside, it is still true that the person who demonstrates good management at the lower level is far more likely to be chosen for a position of greater responsibility.

In the following passage from Luke's Gospel, note the word Jesus uses four times:

> He who is faithful in a very little thing is faithful also in much; and he who is unrighteous in a very little thing is unrighteous also in much. Therefore if you have not been faithful in the use of unrighteous wealth, who will entrust the true riches to you? And if you have not been faithful in the use of that which is another's, who will give you that which is your own? (Luke 16:10-12).

Faithful. ". . . faithful in a very little thing . . . ." In the parable of the talents it was the "good and faithful slave" whom the master commended and promoted. Earlier, Jesus had said,

> For this reason you must also be ready; for the Son of Man is coming at an hour when you do not think He will. Who then is **the faithful and sensible slave** whom his master put in charge of his household to give them their food at the proper time? Blessed is that slave whom his master finds so doing when he comes. Truly I say to you that he will put him in charge of all his possessions (Matthew 24:44-47, emphasis added).

As Paul wrote, ". . . it is required of stewards that one be found trustworthy" (1 Corinthians 4:2). A steward is "one employed in a large household or estate to manage domestic concerns (as the supervision of servants, collection of rents, and keeping of accounts)."[158] The steward is a manager of that which belongs to another. Paul calls an elder "God's steward" (Titus 1:7). The church belongs to the Chief Shepherd; the elders (also called overseers/bishops/pastors in the New Testament) are His under-shepherds on a congregational level (Acts 14:23; 20:17, 28; Philippians 1:1; 1 Peter 5:1-4). But we are all stewards. Each of us has been entrusted by God with money, talents, opportunities, responsibilities, etc. We are stewards, but the only question is: Are we the kind of stewards the Lord would call "good and faithful"?

> As each one has received a special gift, employ it in serving one another as **good stewards of the manifold grace of God.** Whoever speaks, is to do so as one who is speaking the utterances of God; whoever serves is to do so as one who is serving by the strength which God supplies; so that in all things God may be glorified through Jesus Christ, to whom belongs the glory and dominion forever and ever. Amen (1 Peter 4:10-11, emphasis added).

How Important Is It?

If you were looking for someone to manage your finances or rental property, how important would it be to you that the person you hire is honest, trustworthy, and dependable—or as the Bible says, "faithful"? If we learned from an applicant's previous employer that he had been in the habit of taking home from the office small items like pens and sheets of computer paper, would we overlook the theft because it didn't amount to all that much? Is it any different with God? Think of all He entrusts to our care: time, talents, money, health, family, job, etc. God owns it all; our responsibility is to take good care of what is His. Someday we must give Him an account of our stewardship. If we prove faithful with a little, then He will entrust us with more. After stating the principle which is the subject of this chapter, Jesus asked,

Therefore if you have not been faithful in the use of unrighteous wealth, who will entrust the true riches to you? And if you have not been faithful in the use of that which is another's, who will give you that which is your own? (Luke 16:11-12).

Good and Faithful

There is no substitute for plain, good old-fashioned faithfulness. Marriages depend on it. Employers value it in their personnel. And the Lord expects it of His servants.

A synonym for faithful is *dependable*. The dependable person is someone you can count on, regardless. He keeps his promises, he fulfills his obligations, and he doesn't make excuses, nor does he need to. He's always where he's supposed to be, rain or shine. Without dependable people, our society would collapse in a heartbeat.

Faithful Christians are loyal and dependable—loyal to Christ and His church and dependable to do their part. They are there whenever the church assembles. They give regularly and make up missed contributions when ill or out-of-town. If they agree to do a certain job, you don't have to worry—it will get done. They are not one way on Sundays, and entirely different on Mondays. They're genuine. They may not be extroverted or super-talented, but they're faithful, and that's what counts.

Because their loyalty is first and foremost to Jesus Christ as Lord, faithful Christians are willing to suffer through tough times and not quit. They don't require being constantly coddled or pampered—they'd be faithful even if never recognized for their good works. They appreciate a word of encouragement just as anyone would, but they don't let a lack of appreciation keep them from serving the Lord, day in, day out. For them, it will be sufficient reward just to hear the Lord say someday, "Well done, good and faithful slave. **You were faithful with a few things, I will put you in charge of many things; enter into the joy of your master**" (Matthew 25:23, emphasis added).

Questions:

1. Give examples from everyday life that being "faithful in little things" is vitally important.

2. The Bible teaches that "God is faithful" (Deuteronomy 7:9; Isaiah 49:7; 2 Corinthians 1:18). What are some ways in which God Himself is faithful even in little things?

3. Although building Noah's ark was a huge undertaking, to what extent did small details contribute to "the salvation of his household" (Hebrews 11:7)?

4. What is there about human nature that tends to discount small things?

5. What qualities of character do we demonstrate when we give attention to details?

6. What factors are involved in stewardship as demonstrated both in everyday life and in the Scriptures?

CHAPTER 12

Use It or Lose It

**For whoever has, to him more shall be given,
and he will have an abundance; but whoever does not have,
even what he has shall be taken away from him.**

(Matthew 13:12)

R ecently I was on the campus of my alma mater and ran into
my French professor, whom I hadn't seen in over 40 years.
I'm glad he didn't ask if I had kept up my French. Most of what I
learned during those two years in his class I've forgotten. That's
not his fault. I rarely meet anyone who speaks French, so there
hasn't been much opportunity to use what I learned. Ideally, a
couple of years in France after graduation would have greatly
reinforced what I gained in the classroom. But I lost what I had
gained because I didn't use it.

The Principle as Jesus Taught It

We've already examined the parable of the talents in the previous
chapter. In another quite similar parable (Luke 19:11-27), Jesus
told of a nobleman who entrusted ten slaves with one mina each.
A mina was "equal to about 100 days' wages." [159]

When the time came for each of them to report to the master,
the first had multiplied his mina by ten—an increase of one
thousand percent! "Well done, good slave," his master said,
"because you have been faithful in a very little thing, you are to
be in authority over ten cities." Another slave quintupled his—he
was granted five cities.

But then a third slave admitted he had done absolutely nothing
with his mina. Labeling him "worthless," the master ordered,
"Take the mina away from him and give it to the one who has
the ten minas." "Master," someone objected, "he has ten minas
already." The master replied, "I tell you that to everyone who has,

more shall be given, but from the one who does not have, even what he does have shall be taken away." The master knew that the unused mina would multiply in the hands of the one who had already demonstrated what he could do with just one mina.

Among the lessons we can learn from this story is this: What we do today, this very day, with the resources God has given us has direct bearing on how the Lord evaluates us on *that* Day. The productive servants accomplished what they did over the long haul by being diligent daily. A successful life is the sum total of a long series of productive days. But at the end of each one of the unproductive servant's days, could he point to one single thing he had accomplished with his master's money? Another day wasted. And another. And another. And another. What is a wasted life but the sum total of a long series of wasted days, squandered moments, neglected opportunities?

How does this principle work in everyday life and in the spiritual realm? Barclay writes,

> If a man plays a game, if he goes on practicing at it, he will play it with ever greater efficiency; if he does not, he will lose even the small knack and ability he had. If we discipline and train our bodies they will grow ever fitter and stronger; if we do not they grow fat and flabby, and we lose even the strength we had . . . . If we really strive after goodness, if we master this and that temptation, new vistas and new heights of goodness are ever open to us; if we give up the battle and take the easy way even the resistance power we once possessed will be lost and we will slip from even the little height to which we had attained. There is no such thing as standing still in the Christian life.[160]

Ears Are for Hearing

Another passage illustrating the use-it-or-lose-it principle is found in connection with Jesus' story about the sower who scattered his seed on various kinds of soil. This parable is about receptivity to truth. Jesus draws a stark contrast between those who hear but don't understand the gospel and those who not only understand it but bear much fruit as a result. After explaining the parable to His disciples, Jesus said, "If anyone has ears to hear, let him hear," and then stated the principle:

> Take care what you listen to. By your standard of measure it will be measured to you; and more will be given you besides. For whoever has, to him more shall be given; and whoever does not have, even what he has shall be taken away from him (Mark 4:23-25).

Perhaps Jesus' most commonly repeated saying was, "He who has ears, let him hear."[161] In other words, "Pay attention!" This is the opposite of "In one ear and out the other." In practical terms, it means truly absorbing Jesus' words and acting on them. Since Jesus said it so many times, not only must it be tremendously important, but it also exposes a common failure on the part of many of His disciples then and now—a careless neglect or a deliberate ignoring of His word. Can we truly say, "I'm all ears"? Are we like the young Samuel, who was willing to tell the Lord, "Speak, for Your servant is listening" (1 Samuel 3:10)? Or are we like those of the opposite attitude in Isaiah's day: "Let us hear no more about the Holy One of Israel" (Isaiah 30:11b)?

Eyes That Don't See and Ears That Don't Hear

After Jesus told the parable of the sower, His disciples asked Him, "Why do You speak to them in parables?" Jesus explained:

> To you it has been granted to know the mysteries of the kingdom of heaven, but to them it has not been granted. **For whoever has, to him more shall be given, and he will have an abundance; but whoever does not have, even what he has shall be taken away from him.** Therefore I speak to them in parables; because while seeing they do not see, and while hearing they do not hear, nor do they understand . . . . But blessed are your eyes, because they see; and your ears, because they hear. For truly I say to you that many prophets and righteous men desired to

see what you see, and did not see it, and to hear what you hear, and did not hear it (Matthew 13:10-13, 16-17, emphasis added; see Acts 28:23-28).

The principle in bold print above could be paraphrased: "For whoever has the desire to know the truth, to him more shall be given, and he will have an abundance—more truth, a deepened ability to understand; but whoever does not have, who lacks the inclination to learn, even what little he has will be taken away from him."

In a sermon, Alexander Maclaren expressed his frustration with those in his congregation "who have been listening, listening, listening, until your systems have become so habituated to this Christian preaching that it does not produce the least effect. It runs off you like rain off waterproof." [162]

On the positive side of the principle, William Hendriksen offers this encouraging insight:

> Whoever has, to him shall be given. The disciples (exception Judas Iscariot) had "accepted Jesus." With reference to them he was later on going to say to the Father, "They have kept thy word" (John 17:6) and "They are not of the world" (17:16). To be sure, this faith was accompanied by many a weakness, error, and flaw. But the beginning had been made. Therefore, according to heaven's rule, further progress was assured, an advance in knowledge, love, holiness, joy, etc., in all the blessings of the kingdom of heaven, for salvation is an ever deepening stream (Ezekiel 47:1-5). Every blessing is a guarantee of further blessings to come (John 1:16): "he shall have abundantly." [163]

Why Some Are Spiritually Hearing Impaired

Years ago, our son was in a group of boys putting on a skit for their parents. Holding his hands over his eyes, one of the boys cried out, "I can't see! I can't see!" Another asked, "Why not?" The first boy replied, "I've got my eyes closed."

Some people don't see because they choose not to. Jeremiah complained,

To whom shall I speak and give warning
That they may hear?
Behold, their ears are closed
And they cannot listen.
Behold, the word of the LORD has become a reproach to them;
They have no delight in it (Jeremiah 6:10; see 5:21; 6:17; Ezekiel 12:2).

But why would anyone not delight in the Lord's Word? A child ignores his mother's call to come in for a nap because: a) he's having too much fun playing, or b) he hates naps, or c) he can't stand being told what to do, or d) he is so absorbed in his play that the call doesn't even register in his consciousness, or e) he is afraid his playmates might make fun of him for being a "mama's boy," or f) a combination of the above. For adults, the love of sin and an unwillingness to repent are so often the hidden agenda of unbelief. Note the common thread running through the following passages.

This is the judgment, that the Light has come into the world, and **men loved the darkness rather than the Light**, for their deeds were evil. **For everyone who does evil hates the Light, and does not come to the Light for fear that his deeds will be exposed** (John 3:19-20, emphasis added).

Why do you not understand what I am saying? It is because you cannot hear My word. **You are of your father the devil, and you want to do the desires of your father** . . . . He who is of God hears the words of God; for this reason you do not hear them, because you are not of God (John 8:43-44, 47).

For the wrath of God is revealed from heaven against all ungodliness and unrighteousness of men **who suppress the truth in unrighteousness**, because that which is known about God is evident within them; for God made it evident to them. For since the creation of the world His invisible attributes, His eternal power and divine nature, have been clearly seen, being understood through what has been made, so that they are without excuse. For even though they knew God, they did not honor Him as God or give thanks, but they became futile in their speculations, and their foolish heart was darkened . . . . And just as **they did not see fit to acknowledge God any longer,** God gave them over to a depraved mind, to do those things which are not proper . . . (Romans 1:18-21, 28).

So this I say, and affirm together with the Lord, that you walk no longer just as the Gentiles also walk, in the futility of their mind, **being darkened in their understanding,** excluded from the life of God because of the ignorance that is in them, because of the hardness of their heart; and they, having become callous, **have given themselves over to sensuality for the practice of every kind of impurity with greediness** (Ephesians 4:17-19).

Then that lawless one will be revealed . . . the one whose coming is in accord with the activity of Satan, with all power and signs and false wonders, and with all the deception of wickedness, for those who perish, because **they did not receive the love of the truth** so as to be saved. For this reason God will send upon them a deluding influence so that they will believe what is false, in order that they all may be judged **who did not believe the truth, but took pleasure in wickedness** (2 Thessalonians 2:8-12).

For the time will come when they will not endure sound doctrine; but **wanting to have their ears tickled, they will accumulate for themselves teachers in accordance to their own desires,** and will turn away their ears from the truth and will turn aside to myths (2 Timothy 4:3-4; see Isaiah 30:9-11).

To paraphrase this last passage, *Tell me what I want to hear. Talk to me about redemption, not repentance; happiness, not holiness; rights, not responsibilities; self-esteem, not self-denial; crown-wearing, not cross-bearing.*

William Barclay comments:

There are many things which can shut a man's mind. Prejudice can make a man blind to everything he does not wish to see. The unteachable spirit can erect a barrier which cannot easily be broken down. The unteachable spirit can result from one of two things. It can be the result of pride that does not know that it needs to know; and it can be the result of fear of new truth, and the refusal to adventure on the ways of thought. Sometimes an immoral character and a man's way of life can shut his mind. There may be truth which condemns the things he loves . . . and many a man refuses to listen or to recognize the truth which condemns him, for there are none so blind as those who deliberately will not see.[164]

Eyes and ears are our main truth receptors. If we don't want to see something, all we have to do is shut our eyes. Our ears, however, have no such ability. Or do they? Though our ears are not designed to close, physically, our mind is quite capable of shutting out any unwanted messages. We may even become quite adept at tuning out unwelcome truth.

Pilate's Question

At His trial before Pilate, Jesus told him, "Everyone who is of the truth hears my voice." Pilate then asked, "What is truth?" (John 18:37-38). Merrill Tenney says of Pilate's question, "Was it facetious, scornful, impatient, despairing, or sincere? Even from the context it is not possible to be sure what he meant."[165] Yet is clear that he knew at least two truths: 1) he knew that Jesus was innocent—and repeatedly said so (Luke 23:13-15, 20-22), and 2) he knew that Jesus' accusers were motivated by envy of Him (Matthew 27:18). Yet in spite of these two truths, *which he knew*, he went ahead and let them crucify Him. By this injustice, he acted against the truth he already possessed. With embodied Truth Himself standing right there in front of him, Pilate asked, "What is truth?"—but he didn't wait for Jesus' reply. Commenting on this incident, Francis Bacon wrote, "What is truth? said jesting Pilate, and would not stay for an answer."[166]

Was Pilate's question merely facetious, as Bacon suggests? Quite possibly. Another view is that he was momentarily distracted.[167]

Whatever his motive for not waiting for Jesus' response, Pilate forfeited whatever truth he knew, thus losing any benefit he might have received from the One who had told His disciples the night before, "I am the way, and the *truth*, and the life; no one comes to the Father but through Me" (John 14:6, italics added).

"What is truth?" David T. Lusk observes,

> . . . Pilate asked the only man in the world who could have ever answered that question, but didn't even wait for an answer. He wasn't expecting an answer. The truth could have been his had he wanted it but he turned and went out on the porch.
>
> But that in itself fulfilled the statement that Jesus had made . . . "I have come into the world, to testify to the truth. Everyone who is of the truth hears My voice." Pilate did not choose to hear his voice and therefore showed that he was not of the truth. He was not of it, so he could not find it.[168]

In One Ear . . .

Years later, Felix, who held the same governor's office Pilate had once occupied, was given the opportunity on numerous occasions to hear the apostle Paul. "But as he [Paul] was discussing righteousness, self-control and the judgment to come, Felix became frightened and said, 'Go away for the present, and when I find time I will summon you'" (Acts 24:25). The truth was hitting home—hard! Felix understood only too well what the truth was demanding of him—to repent—but that was more than he was willing to do. And so he told Paul, "Go away for the present . . . ." As far as we know, he never obeyed the truth he heard Paul preach.

Then there are those who seem quite willing to listen, but that's as far as it goes.

> For Herod himself had sent and had John arrested and bound in prison on account of Herodias, the wife of his brother Philip, because he had married her. For John had been saying to Herod, "It is not lawful for you to have your brother's wife." Herodias had a grudge against him and wanted to put him to death and could not do so; for Herod was afraid of John, knowing that

he was a righteous and holy man, and he kept him safe. And when he heard him, he was very perplexed; *but he used to enjoy listening to him* (Mark 6:17-20, italics added).

Eager to listen—wicked in spite of it.

Good Listeners

In refreshing contrast, there were others who were eager to listen and obey. Here are two examples from the Old Testament and two from the New:

1) When Josiah, king of Judah, heard the book of the law read in his presence, he was overwhelmed with grief as he realized how far God's people had drifted from Him. Immediately he set to work leading his people in implementing the words he had heard (2 Kings 22-23). Is it any wonder that when Josiah died, the great prophet Jeremiah lamented his untimely passing (2 Chronicles 35:25)?

2) After the Jewish exiles from Babylonian captivity returned to Jerusalem, few of them had a copy of God's Word. They asked Ezra, the scribe, to read it to them. As he unrolled the scroll, the people stood in reverence, and for several hours they paid close attention as he read. In the days that followed, when the people of Judah learned what God required of them, they obeyed. They pledged themselves "to walk in God's law . . . and to keep and to observe all the commandments of GOD . . ." (Nehemiah 10:29).

3) As he journeyed home toward Ethiopia, the queen's treasurer was reading aloud from the book of Isaiah when Philip, the evangelist, approached him. The Ethiopian readily accepted his help in understanding the passage that had so puzzled him. It was the fifty-third chapter of Isaiah, the greatest prophecy of the death of Jesus in the Old Testament, written seven centuries before the cross. When the Ethiopian understood enough to make a response to what he had learned about Jesus, he was eager to be baptized right then and there by the side of the road. After

emerging from the water, he "went on his way rejoicing" (Acts 8:26-39).

4) Cornelius, whose prayer life we studied in Chapter 7, was anxiously awaiting Peter's arrival. As Peter entered his house, he found a large number of Cornelius's family and friends whom he had invited for this special occasion. Cornelius told him about the angel who had instructed him to send for Peter. "So I sent for you immediately, and you have been kind enough to come. Now then, we are all here present before God to hear all that you have been commanded by the Lord" (Acts 10:33). Peter then preached, and before the end of the day Cornelius and his household were disciples of Christ.

In all four of these cases, we see people whose ears were attuned to the Word of God. They took it seriously and obeyed it eagerly. They truly had ears to hear.

Do we?

Questions:

1. The first half of the use-it-or-lose-it principle is a promise, and the second half is a warning. When and how do the promise and the warning find their fulfillment?

2. We looked at passages indicating the "hidden agenda of unbelief." On the opposite side, why do others love and seek the truth?

3. Since our lives are either productive or wasted, depending on how we use our time, how can we use today to the greatest advantage?

4. What can we learn about being truth-seekers from the Bereans? (Acts 17:10-12)

5. What are the costs of seeking truth?

6. What are the costs of not seeking the truth?

CHAPTER 13

God Responds to Us as We Respond to Him

**Therefore everyone who confesses Me before men,
I will also confess him before My Father who is in heaven.
But whoever denies Me before men, I will also deny him
before My Father who is in heaven.**

(Matthew 10:32-33)

When I was a boy, I had one of those plastic puzzles about three inches square with small tongue-and-groove tiles you could slide either vertically or horizontally until you had them all in the right order, whether it was a picture or a worded message. I never discovered the technique for doing this quickly, but once in awhile after much trial and error, I was able to get all the tiles into place.

One puzzle I specifically recall was based on the words of James 4:8, "Draw near to God and He will draw near to you" (I think the puzzle used the King James wording, "Draw nigh to God, and he will draw nigh to you.") As a result of working this puzzle repeatedly more than a half century ago, this verse made a lasting impression on my mind. It makes a great memory verse, but an even greater guide for living.

James 4:8 is a wonderfully encouraging promise; but if we study it in its context (vv. 1-10), we find it surrounded by severe reprimands. James is taking Christians to task for compromising their devotion to God by being chummy with the world. "Therefore whoever wishes to be a friend of the world makes himself an enemy of God" (James 4:4; see 1 John 2:15-17). We can't have it both ways, James says. God and the world are mutually exclusive. By choosing the world we push God away, but when we draw near to Him, putting the world behind us, He moves in our direction.

Over and over we run into this principle in Scripture. Responding to God as He desires is to our ultimate advantage;

but if we fail to respond, this principle serves as a sober warning. Note how the following passages state the principle in a variety of ways, but all say essentially the same thing:

> . . . those who honor Me I will honor, and those who despise Me will be lightly esteemed (1 Samuel 2:30).

> . . . . the LORD is with you when you are with Him . . . . if you seek Him, He will let you find Him; but if you forsake Him, He will forsake you (2 Chronicles 15:2; see 12:5; 24:20; 1 Chronicles 28:9).

> For the eyes of the LORD move to and fro throughout the earth that He may strongly support those whose heart is completely His (2 Chronicles 16:9).

> The hand of our God is favorably disposed to all those who seek Him, but His power and His anger are against all those who forsake Him (Ezra 8:22).

> "Return to Me," declares the LORD of hosts, "that I may return to you" . . . (Zechariah 1:3; see 2 Chronicles 30:6, 9; Malachi 3:7).

> For whoever is ashamed of Me and My words, the Son of Man will be ashamed of him when He comes in His glory . . . (Luke 9:26).

> Draw near to God and He will draw near to you (James 4:8).

Let's see how these verses look in chart form:

How we respond to God	determines	how He responds to us.
When we confess Christ before men		He confesses us before His Father in heaven.
When we deny Christ before men		He denies us before His Father in heaven.
When we honor God		He honors us.
When we despise God		He lightly esteems us.
When we are with God		He is with us.

How we respond to God	determines	how He responds to us.
When we seek God		He lets us find Him.
When we forsake Him		He forsakes us.
When our heart is completely His		He strongly supports us.
When we seek God		He is favorably disposed toward us.
When we forsake God		His power and anger are against us.
When we return to God		He returns to us.
When we are ashamed of Christ		He is ashamed of us.
When we draw near to God		He draws near to us.

It's hard to miss the point. God is telling us what to expect when we please or displease Him—in either case He will respond accordingly. This relates to what we saw in Chapter 7: God listens to us if we are willing to listen to Him. The passages cited in the chart above can make an even greater impact on our hearts when we study them in their contexts. Let's examine just three of them:

Priests in Name Only

Eli's two sons, Hophni and Phinehas, were priests, but they "were worthless men; they did not know the LORD . . . the sin of the young men was very great before the LORD, for the men despised the offering of the LORD" (1 Samuel 2:12, 17). Priests had a right to designated portions of certain sacrifices brought by the people, but Hophni and Phinehas greedily demanded more than their share. In doing so they made themselves enemies of God. And so God sent a prophet to Eli with this message:

"Why do you kick at My sacrifice and at My offering which I have commanded in My dwelling, and honor your sons above Me, by making yourselves fat with the choicest of every offering of My people Israel?" Therefore the LORD God of Israel declares, "I did indeed say that your house and the house of your father should walk before Me forever"; but now the LORD declares, "Far be it from Me—**for those who honor Me I will honor, and those who despise Me will be lightly esteemed**" (1 Samuel 2:29-30, emphasis added).

As a result, God decreed that Hophni and Phinehas would both die in battle, and the priestly line of Eli would come to an end. The principle in bold print above could stand on its own apart from its context and still teach a powerful truth, but it takes on greater significance when we understand the circumstances that prompted God to say this.

The King Whose Faith Grew Weaker

King Asa is a fascinating case study of both strong faith and weak faith. He illustrates both the positive and negative sides of the principle. He did many good things. He removed idolatry from the land, and he "commanded Judah to seek the LORD God of their fathers and to observe the law and the commandment" (2 Chronicles 14:4). When threatened by an Ethiopian army nearly twice the size of his, Asa prayed:

LORD, there is no one besides You to help in the battle between the powerful and those who have no strength; so help us, O LORD our God, for we trust in You, and in Your name have come against this multitude. O LORD, You are our God; let not man prevail against You (2 Chronicles 14:11).

In response to this fervent petition, God gave victory to Asa's army. Afterward God sent this message through the prophet Azariah:

Listen to me, Asa, and all Judah and Benjamin: the LORD is with you when you are with Him. And if you seek Him, He will let you find Him; but if you forsake Him, He will forsake you . . . . But you, be strong, and do not lose courage, for there is reward for your work (2 Chronicles 15:2, 7).

Asa and the people responded well to these words. "They entered into the covenant to seek the LORD God of their fathers with all their heart and soul . . ." (2 Chronicles 15:12).

But later something happened to Asa's faith. When threatened by King Baasha of North Israel, instead of drawing on prayer-power as he had done before, he played power politics by bribing the king of Aram to fight Baasha. As a result, Baasha stopped building fortifications, and Asa's plan appeared successful—but not in God's eyes. The prophet Hanani came calling on Asa with this stern rebuke:

> Because you have relied on the king of Aram and have not relied on the LORD your God, therefore the army of the king of Aram has escaped out of your hand. Were not the Ethiopians and the Lubim an immense multitude with very many chariots and horsemen? Yet because you relied on the LORD, He delivered them into your hand. For the eyes of the LORD move to and fro throughout the earth that He may strongly support those whose heart is completely His. You have acted foolishly in this. Indeed, from now on you will surely have wars (2 Chronicles 16:7-9).

Imbedded in this reprimand is a tremendous promise: God is actively looking for those He can strongly support—specifically, "those whose heart is completely His." What right-thinking person would not want God's strong support? But to have it, we must qualify. Earlier, Asa did qualify, but this time his heart was not completely His. Therefore he forfeited God's strong support.

Asa showed what he thought of Hanani's rebuke by having him imprisoned. "And Asa oppressed some of the people at the same time" (2 Chronicles 16:10). Three years later, "Asa became diseased in his feet. His disease was severe, yet even in his disease he did not seek the LORD, but the physicians" (2 Chronicles 16:12). Asa was not wrong in using physicians (Matthew 9:12;

Colossians 4:14); his fatal error was in failing to consult the Great Physician.

How can a man lean so strongly on God at one point, but then later resort to human help when faced with a similar threat? It was as though Asa had spiritual amnesia. He forgot his previous prayer, ". . . help us, O Lord our God, for we trust in You . . ." (14:11). He forgot how powerfully God had responded to his prayer of faith. Hanani the prophet, as previously mentioned, reminded Asa of his previous trust, which he subsequently abandoned. The tragedy was that even though God is always ready and willing to help, Asa didn't ask (James 4:2). God did not fail Asa; Asa failed God. How much better would Asa's last years have been with God's help than without? It's easy to find fault with Asa, but do we also sometimes lean on the wrong things?

Drawing Near to the God Who Wants to Draw Near to Us
Now let's return to the passage with which we began: "Draw near to God and He will draw near to you." Perhaps the best illustration of this principle is Jesus' parable of the Prodigal Son in Luke 15. At the beginning of the story, the younger son was antsy to leave home. His father gave him the inheritance he demanded. With cash in hand, he was free! Arriving in what the King James Version calls "the far country," he could enjoy all the pleasures money could buy—until he had run through his entire inheritance. (*prodigal* means wasteful.) His insolvency was then compounded by a famine. The far country was drained dry of all its glamour. No funds, no fun, no food, no friends. He experienced the bitter aftertaste of "the passing pleasures of sin" (Hebrews 11:25). He was alone, broke, and hungry. He had gone from riches to rags. The party was over, and he ended up as a pig-tender—and a very hungry one at that. He had sown to the flesh, and he didn't like the harvest.

"Draw Near to God"

But for all he had lost, there was one thing he still had—his memory. He remembered his father. He thought of home and the abundant food there. The old place he had been so anxious to leave behind now beckoned. Home never looked so good! For the first time he could see the far country, home, and himself in a totally different and more accurate light. The turning point of the story comes "when he came to himself," as the King James Version has it. At this decisive moment, when the fog suddenly lifted, he realized for the first time just how desperate his condition was. Now his thinking was more in line with his father's assessment of him as one who was "dead" and "lost" (v. 32). Even before his thinking cleared, during those heady days of "riotous living" (v. 13 KJV) before his inheritance money ran out, even then the Prodigal was in desperate straits. Even when he was having a high old time in the far country, thoroughly absorbed in the pleasures of sin, especially then, he was spiritually dead and lost. He just didn't know it yet—not until "he came to himself." With this new perspective came the firm resolve: "I will get up and go to my father . . . ."

In making this decision he was exercising his free will. Of his own free will he had chosen to leave home. Of his own free will he chose to return home. At first he desperately wanted what the far country had to offer. But after life turned sour, he strongly desired what home had to offer. The Prodigal proves that we can change our desires. He no longer wanted what he once wanted. And he now wanted what he had once left behind. His heart was ready for something better.

"So he got up and came to his father." "The road to hell," it's often said, "is paved with good intentions." That's true. But there is nothing wrong *per se* with good intentions. All genuinely great accomplishments began as good intentions. Yet we know how easily good intentions fail to translate into good actions. But the Prodigal didn't fall into that trap.

What if he had stayed in the pigpen due to rebellion, pride, shame, or despair? Or what if he kept telling himself, "Someday I will go back to my father. Someday I will!"—but never got around to it? Every day in the pigpen was a day of needless suffering. Every day in the pigpen was a day away from home. Every day in the pigpen was another day wasted.

"The backslider in heart will have his fill of his own ways . . ." (Proverbs 14:14). After years of chemical dependence, an addict finally hits bottom and is willing to admit, "I need help!" Or someone gets so fed up with his insatiable appetite for pornography that he makes up his mind to do whatever it takes to be set free. The unfaithful Christian thinks of his broken promises and what he has forfeited, and he resolves to stop living in disobedience and be restored to faithfulness.

> Let us examine and probe our ways,
> And let us return to the LORD (Lamentations 3:40).

Oh, the value of a made-up mind! When the Prodigal had had enough of his sinful ways, he was ready to repent. For him, repentance meant two things: a) turning his back on the far country, and b) turning his feet toward home.

> I considered my ways
> And turned my feet to Your testimonies (Psalm 119:59).

"And He Will Draw Near to You"

Before reconciliation could take place, the son had to start moving in the father's direction. He went through four stages: 1) unhappy at home, 2) happy to be away, 3) unhappy to be away, and 4) happy to be home. The third stage was the most crucial. It was at this point that he changed his perspective and made up his mind to humble himself. He then had to turn his feet toward home. He had to confess what he had been unwilling to admit before, "Father, I have sinned against heaven and in your sight; I am no longer worthy to be called your son." Unlike the conniver

Absalom, who wanted reconciliation with his father David on his own less-than-honorable terms (2 Samuel 13-14), the Prodigal simply threw himself on his father's mercies.

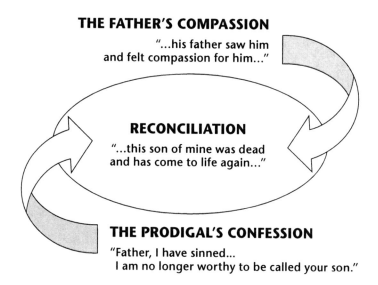

THE FATHER'S COMPASSION
"...his father saw him and felt compassion for him..."

RECONCILIATION
"...this son of mine was dead and has come to life again..."

THE PRODIGAL'S CONFESSION
"Father, I have sinned...
I am no longer worthy to be called your son."

Although the word *grace* does not appear in our story, it's about grace from start to finish. Grace has been defined as getting what we need, not what we deserve. Grace does not condone sin; it forgives sin. Grace is love seeking to heal a broken relationship. Grace is love offering the sinner an opportunity to change.

For the Prodigal, grace meant a robe for the back he had turned toward his father as he left home; ring for the hand that had greedily grasped the inheritance, which he then let slip through his fingers; sandals for the feet that had wandered so far; and feast for the one who had fallen so low.

If the broken relationship between father and son was to be mended, what had to give? They both had to move in the other's direction. Reconciliation between two parties is impossible if neither desires it, or only one does. What had caused the son to leave his father? Selfishness, pride, foolish choices. What made reconciliation possible? First and foremost, the father's love. He never stopped loving. He loved his son before he left, when he was selfish and demanding. He loved him when he was far from home, living in rebellion and sin. He loved him when he came home smelling of the pigsty. The son was out of money, out of food, out of friends, but never out of his father's love. The son's heart was not always turned toward his father, but the father's heart was always turned toward his son. The father's love is the one positive constant in the story. It is his love that made reconciliation possible. As Ronald A. Ward observed, "The first step in man's salvation is taken by God, because to draw near to God is itself a response to His prior call."[169]

The Father's Heart

Even though we call it the parable of the Prodigal Son, the main character in Jesus' story is not the son, but the father. It is noteworthy that when the father saw his son approaching in the distance, he "felt compassion for him" (v. 20). This is the same word so often used of Jesus (Matthew 9:36; 14:14; 15:32; 20:34; Mark 1:41; Luke 7:13). By attributing compassion to the father of the Prodigal, Jesus was saying that the father reflected His own heart toward the lost. And just as Jesus didn't just feel compassion but showed it, so the father's compassionate heart was then translated into compassionate action:

> But the father said to his slaves, "Quickly bring out the best robe **and** put it on him, **and** put a ring on his hand **and** sandals on his feet; **and** bring the fattened calf, kill it, **and** let us eat and celebrate . . . (Luke 15:22-23, emphasis added).

It seems the father couldn't do enough! He kept thinking of more and more ways to show his love, express his joy, and welcome his long-lost son. And this was after he had run out to welcome him with an embrace and kiss. How it thrills God when one of His long-lost children comes home! It is significant that the last word of the story is *found*.

Why This Story?

Jesus told this story, along with the parables of the lost sheep and the lost coin, to counter the complaint of those who could not comprehend why Jesus spent so much time with society's rejects (Luke 15:1-3). The Pharisees contemptuously called them "sinners." Sinners they were, but so were the Pharisees. The Pharisees' sins were not the same as those whom they despised, but they were sinners all. Jesus' strongest rebukes were reserved for these religious leaders, whom He exposed as hypocrites. The critical elder brother in the latter part of the parable depicts just how ugly and cold-hearted Pharisaic self-righteousness can be. When the Pharisees heard Jesus tell this story, did they recognize themselves in the character of the loveless elder brother?

In contrast, the tax collectors and sinners, like the Prodigal, were humble, penitent, and open to change. Jesus chose even the despised tax collector Matthew as one of His apostles, and He invited Himself to be a guest in the home of Zacchaeus, who was not just a tax collector, but a chief tax collector. Those who castigated Jesus as "a friend of tax collectors and sinners" (Matthew 11:19) neither understood Him nor the heart of His Father. Jesus was and still is the friend of sinners. What the Pharisees meant as a negative is one of the most positive things that can be said about Jesus. If He were not a friend of sinners, where would that leave us?

Although the Prodigal's chief sin was self-indulgence, the elder brother was guilty of self-righteousness. Both were unworthy of a father like that. The elder brother didn't understand his father's love for his younger brother. He didn't understand grace. He thought in terms of deserving/undeserving and worthy/unworthy. He just didn't get it.

But the Prodigal, who failed at first to appreciate his father's love, came to enjoy a degree of fellowship with his father that his elder brother never had and perhaps never would. The Prodigal repented while the elder brother resented. The Prodigal humbled himself; the elder brother exalted himself. The Prodigal was willing to admit, "I was wrong." The elder brother said of his sibling, "He was wrong," and to his father, "You are wrong!" The Prodigal said, "I am unworthy," while the elder brother said, "I deserve better."

First Step Toward Home

Perhaps the story of the Prodigal fits you perfectly. On the other hand, you may have difficulty identifying with this young man because you haven't walked on the wild side. Could it be, however, that your "far country" is being so caught up in work and family and recreation (good things in themselves) that you have no time for God? Or maybe your far country is one of apathy or envy or materialism—or pride. In other words, wherever you are, if it's not home, then do you realize that you are "dead" and you are "lost"? Isn't it time—way past time—to come to yourself, and then go to your Father?

If you make this freewill choice, as the Prodigal did, what can you expect from your Father in heaven?

> He who conceals his transgressions will not prosper, but he who confesses and forsakes them will find *compassion* (Proverbs 28:13, italics added).

Imagine a different scenario. What if the father had sat on his porch, arms crossed, scowling as his son approached, impatiently tapping his foot? "Where have you been all this time? Just look at you! You're filthy. You stink! You've got a lot of nerve showing your face around here! I know you—you've been up to no good, haven't you? Didn't I tell you you'd never amount to anything? And where's that inheritance I gave you? Blew it all, didn't you? If you think I'm giving you another dime, you've got another thing coming!"

But the father came running.

Questions:

1. Which of God's character qualities does this principle demonstrate?

2. What kind of God would God be if He made no distinctions between those who respond favorably toward Him and those who do not?

3. Why, do you suppose, is this principle stated so often in the Bible?

4. What is there in human nature that tends to rebel against this principle?

5. How did God apply the principle in dealing with King Saul? (1 Samuel 15—note especially vv. 23, 26)

6. What is there about the parable of the Prodigal Son that is so compelling?

Notes

1   Leon Morris, *The New Bible Commentary: Revised*, ed. D. Guthrie and J. A. Moyter (Grand Rapids, MI: Wm. B. Eerdmans Publishing Co., 1973), 1272.

2   Henry Eli Speck Sr, "The Relationship of God's Natural and Spiritual Worlds," *Abilene Christian College Bible Lectures* (Austin, TX: Firm Foundation Publishing House, 1939), 96.

3   M. H. Cressey, *The Illustrated Bible Dictionary*, Vol. 2, ed. J. D. Douglas (Leicester, England: Inter-Varsity Press, 1980), 1009.

4   Taken from "Great Is Thy Faithfulness" by Thomas O. Chisholm. © 1923. Ren. 1951 Hope Publishing Co., Carol Stream, IL 60188. All rights reserved. Used by permission.

5   Howard G. Hendricks and William D. Hendricks, *Living by the Book: The Art and Science of Reading the Bible* (Chicago, IL: Moody Publishers, 2007), 352.

6   Stephen R. Covey, *The Seven Habits of Highly Effective People: Restoring the Character Ethic* (New York: Simon and Schuster, 1989), 122-123.

7   Speck, 97.

8   Joe R. Barnett, "The Ultimate 'How To' Book" [tract] (Lubbock, TX: Pathway Publishing House, 1982), 6.

9   Carroll B. Ellis, "Solomon, Practice What You Preach!" *Power for Today* (May/June 1988): 65.

10 *answers.yahoo.com* › ... › *Science & Mathematics* › *Astronomy & Space*.

11 Taken from *Disappointment with God: Three Questions No One Asks Aloud* by Philip Yancey, 145. Copyright © 1988 by Philip Yancey. Use by permission of Zondervan. www.Zondervan.com.

12 Joe R. Barnett, *Live! With Peace, Power and Purpose*, The 20th Century Sermon Series (Abilene, TX: Biblical Research Press, 1978), 90.

13 *The Pursuit of Holiness* by Jerry Bridges, 32. © 1978. Used by Permission of NavPress. All Rights Reserved. *www.navpress.com* (1-800-366-7788).

14 *Our Daily Bread* (January/February 1884): January 20.

15 Alexander Maclaren, *Maclaren's Expositions of Holy Scripture*, Vol. 4 (Grand Rapids, MI: Wm. B. Eerdmans Publishing Company, 1959), 113.

16 Maclaren, 116.

17 Wayne W. Dyer, *Pulling Your Own Strings* (New York: Thomas Y. Crowell Company, 1978), 184.

18 Tommy South, "I Have Sinned," *Gospel Advocate* (August 2006): 30.

19 James Burton Coffman, *Commentary on Romans* (Abilene, TX: ACU Press, 1984), 231.

20 Phillip D. O'Hern, "Seeing God's Plan," *Power for Today* (March/April 1988): March 10.

21 Cecil May III, "The No-Change List," *Bulletin Digest* Oct. 2011: 13.

22 Charles B. Hodge, Jr., "Grace Demands Wrath" (Little Rock, AR: The Keynoter, bulletin of the Sixth and Izard Church of Christ, January 16, 1986).

23 G. C. Brewer, *Christ Crucified: A Book of Sermons Together with a Lecture on Evolution* (Cincinnati, OH: Christian Leader Corporation, 1928), 89.

24 James Denney, *The Death of Christ*, Biblical Classics Library (Carlisle, Cumbria, England: Paternoster Press, 1997), 107.

25 R. E. Nixon, *The New Bible Commentary: Revised*, ed. D. Guthrie and J. A. Moyter (Grand Rapids, MI: Wm. B. Eerdmans Publishing Co., 1973), 825.

26 William Barclay, *The Gospel of Matthew*, Vol. 1, The Daily Study Bible (Philadelphia, PA: The Westminster Press, 1958), 252.

27 R. A. Torrey, *How to Pray* (New York: Fleming H. Revell Co., 1900), 84.

28 N. Lamar Reinsch, Jr., "The Contemporary Christian and Materialism," *Firm Foundation* (December 14, 1971): 790.

29 Foy E. Wallace, *The Sermon on the Mount and the Civil State* (Nashville, TN: Foy E. Wallace Jr. Publications, 1967), 68.

30 Taken from *Generous Living: Finding Contentment Through Generous Giving* by Ron Blue with Jodie Berndt, 34. Copyright © 1997 by Ronald W. Blue. Use by permission of Zondervan. www.Zondervan.com.

31 William Barclay, *The Gospel of Matthew*, Vol. 1, The Daily Study Bible (Philadelphia, PA: The Westminster Press, 1958), 261.

32 Zig Ziglar, *Confessions of a Happy Christian* (Gretna, LA: Pelican Publishing, Inc., 1978), 123.

33 G. Campbell Morgan, "Righteousness or Revenue," *20 Centuries of Great Preaching: An Encyclopedia of Preaching*, Vol. 8, ed. Clyde E. Fant, Jr. and William M. Pinson, Jr. (Waco, TX: Word Books, Publisher, 1971), 27.

34 Eldred Echols, *Discovering the Pearl of Great Price: The Parables of Jesus* (Fort Worth, TX: Sweet Publishing, 1992), 77.

35 Frank L. Cox, *According to Luke* (Austin, TX: Firm Foundation Publishing House, 1941), 50.

36 Richard J. Foster, *Money, Sex & Power: The Challenge of the Disciplined Life* (San Francisco, CA: Harper & Row, Publishers, 1985), 35.

37 Taken from *The Expositor's Bible Commentary*, Vol. 8, 178-179. Copyright © 1980 by The Zondervan Corporation. Use by permission of Zondervan. www.Zondervan.com.

38 Alexander Maclaren, *Maclaren's Expositions of Holy Scripture*, Vol. 11 (Grand Rapids, MI: Wm. B. Eerdmans Publishing Company, 1959), 248.

39 Taken from *The NIV Study Bible*, ed. by Kenneth Barker, 1908. Copyright © 1985 by The Zondervan Corporation. Use by permission of Zondervan. www.Zondervan.com.

40 A. Plummer, *The Pulpit Commentary*, ed. H. D. M. Spence and Joseph S. Exell, Vol. 22 (Grand Rapids, MI: Wm. B. Eerdmans Publ. Co., 1962), 4.

41 Alexander Maclaren, *Maclaren's Expositions of Holy Scripture*, Vol. 11 (Grand Rapids, MI: Wm. B. Eerdmans Publishing Company, 1959), 249.

42 J. W. Roberts, *The Letters of John* (Austin, TX: R. B. Sweet Company, Inc., 1968), 32.

43 Maclaren, 257.

44 James Burton Coffman, *Commentary on James, 1 & 2 Peter, 1, 2 & 3 John, Jude* (Abilene, TX: ACU Press, 1984), 362.

45 Roberts, 32.

46 John R. W. Stott, *The Epistles of John: An Introduction and Commentary* (Grand Rapids, MI: Wm. B. Eerdmans Publishing Company, 1981), 79.

47 Theodor Haeckel, *Journal in the Night*, translated from the German by Alexander Dru (New York: Pantheon Books, 1950), 42, Item 175.

48 Taken from *The NIV Study Bible*, ed. by Kenneth Barker, 1825. Copyright © 1985 by The Zondervan Corporation. Use by permission of Zondervan. www.Zondervan.com.

49 *Humanist Manifestos I and II*, ed. Paul Kurtz (Buffalo, NY: Prometheus Books, 1973), 16.

50 Joseph Fletcher, *Situation Ethics and the New Morality* (Philadelphia, PA: The Westminster Press, 1966), 146.

51 Laura Sauer, "Mother's Perspective: Living Together Before Marriage is a Must" www.voices.yahoo.com/mothers-perspective-living-together-marriage-111...

52 Prudence Gourguechon, MD, "Ten Reasons to Support Gay Marriage" www.psychologytoday.com/blog/.../tenreasons- support-gay-marriage...

53 Asrael Sky, "5 Reasons Why Pornography is Good for Society" www.voices.yahoo.com/5-reasons-whypornography-good-society-35050...

54 "The Liberty to Choose—Liberty Women's Health Care of Queens www.libertywomenshealth.com/rtc.php

55 Derek Humphry, Liberty and Death: A Manifesto Concerning an Individual's Right to Choose to Die www.hemlocksocietysandiego.org/

56 Walter B. Knight, author and compiler, *Knight's Treasury of Illustrations* (Grand Rapids, MI: Wm. B. Eerdmans Publishing Company, 1963), 361.

57 Taken from *The Expositor's Bible Commentary*, Vol. 5, ed. by Frank E. Gaebelein, 106. Copyright © 1986 by The Zondervan Corporation. Use by permission of Zondervan. www.Zondervan.com.

58 *The Great Texts of the Bible*, ed. James Hastings, Vol. XVI (Grand Rapids, MI: Wm. B. Eerdmans Publishing Company), 439-440.

59 L. L. Morris, "Flesh," *The Illustrated Bible Dictionary*, Vol. 1, editor-at-large J. D. Douglas (Leicester, England: Inter-Varsity Press, 1980), 510. For more on flesh vs. Spirit, see Romans 8:5-8, 12-13 and Galatians 5:16-17.

60 G. B. Shelburne III, "If Only . . ." *Power for Today* Sept.-Oct. 2011: Sept. 23.

61 Paul Lauremce Dunbar, "The Debt," *The Complete Poems of Paul Laurence Dunbar* (New York: Dodd, Mead & Company, 1976), 348.

62 Cecil May III, "The No-Change List," *Bulletin Digest* Oct. 2011: 13.

63 James Allen, *As a Man Thinketh* (including *Morning and Evening Thoughts*) (Mineola, NY: Dover Publications, Inc., 2007), 10.

64 James Allen, 13-14.

65 Stephen R. Covey, *The Seven Habits of Highly Effective People: Restoring the Character Ethic* (New York: Simon and Schuster, 1989), 22.

66 Covey, 90.

67 Philip E. Hughes, *Paul's Second Epistle to the Corinthians*. The New International Commentary on the New Testament (Grand Rapids, MI: Wm. B. Eerdmans Publishing Co., 1973), 329.

68 William Shakespeare, *Julius Caesar*, IV, iii, 217.

69 Garry Friesen with J. Robin Maxson, *Decision-Making & the Will of God: A Biblical Alternative to the Traditional View* (Portland, OR: Multnomah Press, 1980), 371.

70   T. Pierce Brown, *Pertinent Principles* (Wartrace, TN: T. Perce Brown, n.d.), 7.

71   Robert E. Speer, cited by Paul Lee Tan, *Encyclopedia of 7,700 Illustrations* (Garland, TX: Bible Communications, Inc., 1979), 1357 (#6052).

72   Philip E. Hughes, *Paul's Second Epistle to the Corinthians*. The New International Commentary on the New Testament (Grand Rapids, MI: Wm. B. Eerdmans Publishing Co., 1973), 335.

73   Mac Layton, *How to Build a Great Church* (Searcy, AR: Resource Publications, 1987), 275. Used with permission.

74   Wendell Winkler, *Toward Spiritual Maturity*, "Sound Doctrine for Everyday Living" Series (Tuscaloosa, AL: Winkler Publications, Inc., 1974), 52.

75   Colin Kruse, *The Second Epistle of Paul to the Corinthians: An Introduction and Commentary*, Tyndale New Testament Commentaries (Grand Rapids, MI: William B. Eerdmans Publishing Company, 1989), 164.

76   William Barclay, *The Letters to the Corinthians*, The Daily Study Bible (Philadelphia, PA: The Westminster Press, 1956), 261.

77   Charles Hodge, *An Exposition of the Second Epistle to the Corinthians* (Grand Rapids, MI: Wm. B. Eerdmans Publishing Company, n.d.), 219.

78   Charles Caleb Colton, *Lacon: or Many Things in Few Words Addressed to Those who Think* (London: Longman, Orme, Brown, Green, & Longmans, 1937), 134.

79   *The Poetical Works of Christine Georgina Rossetti with Memoir and Notes &c by William Michael Rossetti* (London: Macmillan and Co., Limited, 1906), 197.

80   A. M. Burton, "The Rewards of Liberality," *Gospel Advocate* Sept. 23 1965: 623.

81   T. Croskery, *The Pulpit Commentary*, Vol. 17, ed. H. D. M. Spence and Joseph S. Excell (Grand Rapids, MI: Wm. B. Eerdmans Publishing Company, 1962), 28.

82   B. Thomas, *The Pulpit Commentary*, Vol. 17, ed. H. D. M. Spence and Joseph S. Excell (Grand Rapids, MI: Wm. B. Eerdmans Publishing Company, 1962), 253.

83   Anonymous, "I Love Thee," *Great Songs of the Church, Number Two with Supplement*, E. L. Jorgenson, compiler (Abilene, TX: Great Songs Press, 1976), #628.

84   Taken from *The Expositor's Bible Commentary*, Vol. 9, ed. Frank E. Gaebelein, 147. Copyright © 1986 by The Zondervan Corporation. Use by permission of Zondervan. *www.Zondeervan.com*.

85   Andrew Murray, *The School of Obedience* (Chicago, IL: Fleming H. Revell Company, 1899), 41.

86   *Great Preachers of Today: Sermons of Frank Pack* (Abilene, TX: Biblical Research Press, 1963), 120-121.

87   C. Michael Moss, *Lord, Sometimes I Don't Feel Saved!: Renewing Our Confidence in Christ* (Webb City, MO: Covenant Publishing, 2002), 39.

88   Leon Morris, *The New Bible Commentary: Revised*, ed. D. Guthrie and J. A. Moyter (Grand Rapids, MI: Wm. B. Eerdmans Publishing Co., 1973), 1271.

89   Walter B. Knight, author and compiler, *Knight's Treasury of Illustrations* (Grand Rapids, MI: Wm. B. Eerdmans Publishing Company,1963), 211.

90   James Russell Lowell, *The Vision of Sir Launfal*, pt. II, st. 8.

91   C. E. W. Dorris in David Lipscomb, *A Commentary on the Gospel of John*, edited, with additional notes, by C. E. W. Dorris (Nashville, TN: Gospel Advocate Company, 1968), 230.

92   C. K. Barrett, *The Gospel According to St. John: An Introduction with Commentary and Notes on the Greek Text*, 2nd ed. (Philadelphia, PA: The Westminster Press, 1978), 461.

93   David Lipscomb, *A Commentary on the Gospel of John*, edited with additional notes, by C. E. W. Dorris (Nashville, TN: Gospel Advocate Company, 1968), 229.

94   Henry T. Blackaby and Claude V. King, *Experiencing God: Knowing and Doing the Will of God* (Nashville, TN: © 2004 by Broadman & Holman Publishers), 248.

95   *Great Preachers of Today: Sermons of Frank Pack* (Abilene, TX: Biblical Research Press, 1963), 124.

96   J. I. Packer, *Knowing God* (Downers Grove, IL: InterVarsity Press, 1973), 120.

97   F. LaGard Smith, *Troubling Questions for Calvinists . . . and All the Rest of Us* (Lynchburg, VA: Cotswold Publishing , 2007), 35-36.

98   Letter to the author, November 17, 2011. For more information see Everett Ferguson's monumental work, *Baptism in the Early Church: History, Theology, and Liturgy in the First Five Centuries* (Grand Rapids, MI: William B. Eerdmans Publishing Company, 2009), 871: index on Titus 3:5.

99   Francis Foulkes, *The Epistle of Paul to the Ephesians: An Introduction and Commentary*, The Tyndale New Testament Commentaries (Grand Rapids, MI: Wm. B. Eerdmans Publishing Co., 1981), 20.

100 *Thomas' Valedictory Sermons*, ed. James R. McGill (Birmingham, AL: A Parchment Press Publication, 1968), 38.

101 Delmar Owens, *Launch Out Into the Deep* (Tulsa, OK: Delmar Owens, 1959), 125.

102 Taken from *The Expositor's Bible Commentary*, Vol. 9, ed. Frank E. Gaebelein, 147. Copyright © 1986 by The Zondervan Corporation. Use by permission of Zondervan. www.Zondervan.com.

103 Mack Lyon, *Continuing Instant In Prayer* (Abilene, TX: Quality Printing Co., Inc., 1966), 62.

104 R. A. Torrey, *How to Pray* (New York: Fleming H. Revell Company, 1900), 41-42.

105 Charles Bigg, *A Critical and Exegetical Commentary on the Epistles of St. Peter and St. Jude*, The International Critical Commentary (Edinburgh: T & T Clark, 1902), 155.

106 In addition, see Isaiah 1:15-17; Jeremiah 14:10-12; Ezekiel 20:3, 31; Hosea 5:3-6; Luke 18:9-14.

107 Torrey, 83.

108 Lyon, 62-63.

109 James M. Tolle, *Prayer* (Pasadena, TX: Haun Publishing Company, 1963), 33.

110 Andrew Murray, *Daily Experience with God* (New Kensington, PA: Whitaker House, 1984), 151.

111 Joe Barnett, "Is God Listening?" *UpReach* (November/December 1984):10.

112 *The Complete Works of E. M. Bounds on Prayer* (Grand Rapids, MI: Baker Book House, 1990), 345.

113 *www.merriam-webster.com*. © 2011 Merriam-Webster, Incorporated.

114 Taken from *The Expositor's Bible Commentary*, Vol. 8, ed. Frank E. Gaebelein, 257. Copyright © 1986 by The Zondervan Corporation. Use by permission of Zondervan. *www.Zondervan.com*.

115 Larry Deason, "*One Step Closer to Jesus: Losing Life, Finding Life*": Lessons in *Genuine Discipleship* (Clifton Park, NY: Life Communications, 1993), 80-81.

116 L. E. Maxwell, *Born Crucified* (Chicago, IL: Moody Press, 1945), 174.

117 William Hendriksen, *New Testament Commentary: Exposition of the Gospel According to Luke* (Grand Rapids, MI: Baker Book House, 1978), 808.

118 Janice Greenleaf, "Going for His Glory," *Power for Today* Sept.-Oct. 2011: Sept. 4.

119 Charles Kingsley, *The Good News of God* (Boston, MA: E. P. Dutton and Company, 1865), 158-159.

120 Alexander Maclaren, "The Blessedness of Giving," *Maclaren's Expositions of Holy Scripture*, Vol. 8 (Grand Rapids: Wm. B. Eerdmans Publishing Company, 1959), 213.

121 J. H. Sammis, "When We Walk with the Lord" (italics added).

122 Kerry Williams, "Intentionally Taking Last Place," *Power for Today* May-June 2011: May 14.

123 Frederick Buechner, *Wishful Thinking: A Theological ABC* (New York: Harper & Row Publishers, 1973), 28.

124 Jimmy Allen, *The American Crisis and Other Sermons* (Searcy, AR: Harding College, 1971), 53.

125 George A. Buttrick, *The Parables of Jesus* (Garden City, NY: Doubleday, Doran & Company, Inc., 1928), 88.

126 *The Great Texts of the Bible*, Vol. VI, ed. James Hastings (Grand Rapids, MI: Wm. B. Eerdmans Publishing Co., n.d.), 82.

127 *en.wikipedia.org/wiki/sennacherib.*

128 "THE ART OF BEING A BIG SHOT" by Howard E. Butt Jr., of Laity Lodge, delivered on February 1, 1963 at the Layman's Leadership Institute in Dallas, TX.

129 Jimmy Allen, *The American Crisis and Other Sermons* (Searcy, AR: Harding College, 1971), 47.

130 Taken from *The Speaker's Sourcebook*, compiled by Eleanor L. Doan. Copyright © 1960 by Zondervan Publishing House, Grand Rapids, Michigan, 127. Use by permission of Zondervan. www.Zondervan.com.

131 Everett F. Harrison, *A Short Life of Christ* (Grand Rapids, MI: Wm. B. Eerdmans Publishing Company, 1968), 261.

132 William Barclay, *The Letters to the Philippians, Colossians, and Thessalonians*, 2nd ed., The Daily Study Bible (Philadelphia, PA: The Westminster Press, 1959), 42.

133 Archibald Thomas Robertson, *Word Pictures in the New Testament*, Vol. IV (Grand Rapids, MI: Baker Book House, 1931), 445.

134 D. L. Moody, *The Overcoming Life* (Chicago, IL: Moody Press, 1984), 82.

135 Larry Deason, "*One Step Closer to Jesus: Losing Life, Finding Life*": Lessons in *Genuine Discipleship* (Clifton Park, NY: Life Communications, 1993), 41-42.

136 Taken from *The Speaker's Sourcebook*, compiled by Eleanor L. Doan. Copyright © 1960 by Zondervan Publishing House, Grand Rapids, Michigan, 127. Use by permission of Zondervan. www.Zondervan.com.

137 Martha Davis, Elizabeth Robbins Eshelman, and Matthew McKay, *The Relaxation & Stress Reduction Notebook* (Oakland, CA: New Harbinger Publications, Inc., 1995), 143, 138, 139.

138 D. Edmond Hiebert, *An Introduction to the New Testament, Volume 2, The Pauline Epistles* (Chicago, IL: Moody Press, 1981), 135.

139 E. Hurndall, *The Pulpit Commentary*, ed. H. D. M. Spence and Joseph S. Exell, Vol. 19 (Grand Rapids, MI: Wm. B. Eerdmans Publ. Co., 1962), 303.

140 Alexander Maclaren, "Strength in Weakness," *Maclaren's Expositions of Holy Scripture*, Vol. 9 (Grand Rapids: Wm. B. Eerdmans Publishing Company, 1959), 82.

141 Charles B. Hodge Jr., "The Issue is Sin—Not Suffering" *Gospel Light* Aug. 1995: 118.

142 Taken from *Hot Tub Religion: Christian Living in a Materialistic World* by J. I. Packer, 206. Copyright © 1987 by J. I Packer . Used by permission of Tyndale House Publishers, Inc. All rights reserved.

143 Taken from *Reaching for the Invisible God: What Can We Expect to Find?* by Philip Yancey, 271. Copyright © 2000 by The Zondervan Corporation. Use by permission of Zondervan. *www.Zondervan.com.*

144 Batsell Barrett Baxter and Harold Hazelip, "Jesus and the Sick", Herald of Truth radio program number 520, August 1977.

145 Norman Hillyer, *The New Bible Commentary*: Revised, ed. D. Guthrie and J. A. Moyter (Grand Rapids, MI: Wm. B. Eerdmans Publishing Co., 1973), 1087.

146 Taken from *Reaching for the Invisible God: What Can We Expect to Find?* by Philip Yancey, 282. Copyright © 2000 by The Zondervan Corporation. Use by permission of Zondervan. *www.Zondervan.com.*

147 Robert P. Mullen, "Looking for Strength," *Power for Today* Sept.-Oct. 2011: Oct. 19.

148 Mack Lyon, "Learning to Lean," *In Search of the Lord's Way* television ministry (May 1998), 61.

149 Alexander Maclaren, "Strength in Weakness," *Maclaren's Expositions of Holy Scripture*, Vol. 9 (Grand Rapids: Wm. B. Eerdmans Publishing Company, 1959), 81.

150 Charles Jefferson, *20 Centuries of Great Preaching: An Encyclopedia of Preaching*, Vol. 7, ed. Clyde E. Fant Jr. and William M. Pinson Jr. (Waco, TX: Word Books, Publisher, 1971), 27. 57.

151 Batsell Barrett Baxter, "Little Things in a Day of Bigness", Herald of Truth radio program number 165, November 1970.

152 *Charles Kingsley: His Letters and Memories of His Life*, ed. Frances Eliza Grenfell Kingsley, 9th ed., Vol. 1 (London: C. Kegan Paul & Co., 1877), 431.

153 Sam Parker and Mac Anderson, 212°: *The Extra Degree* (Naperville, IL: Simple Truths, LLC, 2006), 8-11.

154 William F. Arndt and F. Wilbur Gingrich, *A Greek-English Lexicon of the New Testament and Other Early Christian Literature* (Chicago, IL: The University of Chicago Press, 1957), 670.

155 James Freeman Clarke, *Self-Culture: Physical, Intellectual, Moral, and Spiritual—A Course of Lectures*, 15th ed. (Boston, MA: Tichnor and Company, 1880), 445.

156 Charles Jefferson, *20 Centuries of Great Preaching: An Encyclopedia of Preaching*, Vol. 7, ed. Clyde E. Fant, Jr and William M. Pinson, Jr (Waco, TX: Word Books, Publisher, 1971), 27. 59.

157 James Burton Coffman, *Commentary on Luke* (Abilene, TX: ACU Press, 1975), 319.

158 *www.merriam-webster.com/dictionary/steward.*

159 New American Standard Bible, side-column reference edition (Anaheim, CA: Foundation Publications, Inc., 1996), 129.

160 William Barclay, *The Gospel of Luke*, The Daily Study Bible (Philadelphia, PA: The Westminster Press, 1956), 247-248.

161 Matthew 11:15; 13:9, 43; Mark 4:9, 23; Luke 14:35; Revelation 2:7, 11, 17, 29; 3:6, 13, 22.

162 Alexander Maclaren, "Sodom, Capernaum, Manchester," *Maclaren's Expositions of Holy Scripture*, Vol. 10 (Grand Rapids: Wm. B. Eerdmans Publishing Company, 1959), 144.

163 William Hendriksen, *New Testament Commentary: Exposition of the Gospel According to Matthew* (Grand Rapids, MI: Baker Book House, 1973), 553.

164 William Barclay, *The Gospel of Matthew*, Vol. 2, The Daily Study Bible (Philadelphia, PA: The Westminster Press, 1958), 66-67.

165 Taken from *The Expositor's Bible Commentary*, Vol. 9, ed. by Frank E. Gaebelein, 176. Copyright © 1986 by The Zondervan Corporation. Use by permission of Zondervan. *www.Zondervan.com*.

166 Francis Bacon, *Essays: Of Truth*.

167 Lancelot Andrewes, Sermons: Of the Resurrection (1613), cited in *Dictionary of Quotations*, collected and arranged and with comments by Bergen Evans (New York: Delacorte Press, 1968), 710.

168 David T. Lusk, *Within the Halls of Pilate* (Abilene, TX: Quality Printing, 1983), 34-35.

169 Ronald A. Ward, *New Bible Commentary*: Revised, ed. D. Guthrie and J. A. Moyter (Grand Rapids, MI: Wm. B. Eerdmans Publishing Co., 1973), 1232.v